PATHWAY
TO THE NATIONAL CHARACTER
1830 — 1861

Kennikat Press
National University Publications
Series in American Studies

General Editor
James P. Shenton
Professor of History, Columbia University

Robert Lemelin

PATHWAY
TO THE NATIONAL CHARACTER
1830 — 1861

National University Publications
KENNIKAT PRESS • 1974
Port Washington, N. Y. • London

Manufactured in the United States of America

Published by
Kennikat Press Corp.
Port Washington, N.Y./London

Library of Congress Cataloging in Publication Data

Lemelin, Robert, 1934-
    Pathway to the national character, 1830-1861

    (Kennikat Press national university publications.
Series in American studies)
    Bibliography: p.
    1. United States - - Civilization - - 1783-1865. 2. Na-
tional characteristics, American. 3. United States - -
Description and travel - - 1783-1848 - - History. 4. United
States - - Description and travel - - 1848-1865 - - History.
I. Title.
E165.L57   917.3'03'6   74-80589
ISBN 0-8046-9087-1

To Jolene

CONTENTS

THE GENRE AND THE CULTURE

An antebellum publisher told John L. Stephens that travels sold better than anything he could get hold of and they sold longer, and it is this chance remark which led Stephens into a very successful career as a travel book writer. The travel and descriptive writing produced during the thirty years before the Civil War contains for the student of American cultural history a broad purview of antebellum civilization—its drives, its tone, and its complex of responses to existence. The culture began consciously to wrestle with defining the national character, and this body of literature affords the modern reader an insight into the way the culture taught itself to deal with the reality of its identity.

The travel and descriptive writer holds a special position in the development of the American character. His were our first books, and throughout our early history Americans turned to the genre for information and cultural sustenance. It is appropriate that at the end of our colonial period we are given William Bartram's classic *Travels* (1791). The widespread popularity of the travel and descriptive book on the high and popular culture levels during the antebellum period continued the American affinity to the genre, and because of its popularity it is a very useful source for understanding the development of the American character. One has only to consider how often the most creative writers of the period, Melville, Poe, Thoreau, Emerson, Longfellow, and even in a few short pieces Hawthorne, turned to the genre and turned the genre to their artistic purposes, to be persuaded of the interest, the attention, and the acceptance which the form received. Because of this interest, attention, and acceptance, the mass of antebellum travel and descriptive literature holds the potential for discovering essential patterns of culture locked up in their constructs. It is the purpose of this book to remove the veils and to get at essential cultural designs as valid for understanding ourselves today as they were during the antebellum period.

The pervasive influence of travel and descriptive literature becomes clear when we consider the overall travel and descriptive literature industry. Before breaking down the codes in the books and dissecting the underlying constructs contained within the codes, we must acknowledge that the antebellum era eventually gave us the professional traveler. Men like John L. Stephens and Bayard Taylor described their travels in books and newspapers, and dramatized them, sometimes in costume, on the lecture platform. Antebellum Americans were fascinated by exotic places created by the Stephens and Taylors of the age. The travels of these professionals were available to the masses at a very cheap price in newspapers and in book form. However, there is another side to this travel literature fad which also concerns us here.

Because the first half of the nineteenth century saw revolutionary advances in transportation, great numbers of Americans were suddenly able to travel more widely than ever before in their own country. Americans began calling themselves a nation of nomads. They had a great urge to see their country, and a large number of travel and descriptive books capitalized on that urge. Suddenly many minor American writers, who had been crying for support of their literary efforts, were given a product and a market. Just as mass culture and popular literature were emerging, a large number of travel and descriptive books about the United States were written by Americans primarily for an American audience. This literary phenomenon united itself to the search in the first half of the nineteenth century for cultural self-knowledge, cultural independence, and national identity. Americans yearned for cultural freedom from Europe to complement their recently won political freedom, and the travel and descriptive book became a popular tool through which they could study themselves and define their national identity. The tool was very appropriate. It was well known and tried, but more importantly it had an egalitarian aspect. Anyone might write or keep a journal of his travels.

Travel writers had in their hands, then, a genre whose appeal was extensive and which recommended itself as a practical method of self-realization, of self-appraisal on a personal and a national level. Travel books had a long and popular tradition not only in the colonial period but in western civilization in general. In addition, the travel book genre was very malleable stylistically as well as appropriate intellectually to the national character. The genre presented the character of seriousness and high purpose suited to the nation's self-conscious temper. It was also a very practical genre; it served mundane travel needs. It satisfied a contrary inclination also. The aura of adventure, discovery, and verisimilitude in the travel and descriptive book appealed to the activist, materialistic American mind. It is not surprising, then, to find Bayard Taylor reporting in his 1849 trip to California that nothing but Frémont and other travel books were being read. In an era when the search for cultural identity was intense, antebellum Americans approached travel and descriptive writing with a feeling of national dedication, insight, and vision.

There was good reason to take a firm cultural stance in the matter of the national character, and the reason was embodied in the travel writing of foreign visitors. Between 1830 and 1861 a great number of foreign travelers came to the United States to see how the republican experiment was doing. Increased internal facilities for travel encouraged foreigners to undertake a trip here, and many of them wrote accounts of their travels. Criticism of American life, especially of the kind contained in the accounts of British travelers, got under the American skin, but this criticism also gave Americans an impetus to appraise how the republican experiment was doing from their own perspective—in short, to define their national character in their own travel and descriptive books. British criticism had such an impact that it became typical among Americans at the time to refer to the English abuse of America. Henry T. Tuckerman, an antebellum student of travel literature, told about an impoverished professor who had once lived in America, who found himself in Europe without money, and who was offered by a London publisher a handsome fee to write a lively antidemocratic book about American life and manners. American travel and descriptive writers took it upon themselves to reply to what was believed to be the caustically and opportunistically written books of British travelers. Again, it was indeed fortunate that Americans were overly sensitive to foreign criticism, because as they responded to foreign criticism they took on the more important job of self-appraisal.

Native writers of travel and descriptive books had a precise awareness of the terrain of British criticism and answered British attacks on the American character from very essential standpoints. They complained that never before had so large a population been so uniformly judged en masse and that many indiscriminate generalizations were being made. American travel and descriptive writers made petulant references to ignorant and insolent British commentators who in a Parthian manner hurled attacks at the new republic.

It becomes appropriate, at this point, before going on to define the character of American travels, to fill in more detail regarding the character of foreign criticism. A considerable amount of foreign criticism centered on antebellum manners. The foreign travelers came to this country at a time when the manners which travelers were likely to encounter had decidedly changed from those they might have met or read about during the Revolutionary and early national periods. Previously, Federalist refinement had dominated the scene for foreign travelers, and had given them a favorable impression of the United

States. In the antebellum period Jacksonian democracy and the growing role of the frontier in the nation's life combined to emphasize the rougher habits of the great mass of Americans. Whereas earlier foreign visitors had restricted their travels to the refined circles of the East, now expanded and improved travel facilities made western trips easier, and romanticism led Europeans to demand a look at the West and the frontiersman. Foreign travelers, therefore, came more and more into contact with Americans who had shed or had never seen the more fastidious accoutrements of civilization.

Foreign travelers came here at a tumultuous time, and, according to American travel commentators, failed to look beyond the rough exterior of Americans to notice that a showy affluence and boisterous nationalism resulted from the social climate of a rapidly developing commercial and industrial economy, a booming territorial expansion, and a liberal political atmosphere. Material opportunities were plentiful, and daring was high. American society and the national character reflected these exuberant conditions.

In responding to the foreign criticism of American manners, travel and descriptive writers were not remiss in considering all sides of the national character. First of all, they showed an awareness of national faults and generally did not attempt to gloss them over; they tried for a fair self-evaluation. American commentators complained with a patient understanding of their society about tobacco chewing and spitting, bolting one's food, the lack of reserve, poor posture, a fetish for equality, western braggadocio and extravagant display—all aspects of American life criticized by foreign travelers. William Cullen Bryant, while traveling on a steamboat, told of expert tobacco chewers and spitters who considered their accomplishments a sign of high breeding. These gentlemen had never been forced to hypocritically conceal their talent by the fear of woman, nor had they developed an unmanly restraint in exhibiting it, Bryant interestingly enough observed.

Displaying a sensitivity to the British traveler's criticism of American English, Charles Goodrich, in defending his culture's use of language, found very little variation in the idiom, even among the lowest classes, from Maine to Georgia. No uncouth provincialisms or patois offended the traveler's ear. American commentators granted one found a few localisms and a few slight differences in pronunciation, but only in some states. In many states even frontier farmers were said to speak English with nearly classical purity. American travel writers were surprised to find so many British commentators objecting to the addition by Americans of a few words into their common language.

Some books did chauvinistically defend American manners against foreign criticism, but many American travel and descriptive writers attempted to examine the cultural roots of social conditions. American commentators admitted that egalitarianism had its negative aspects; a democratic society leveled life downward as well as upward. The practical result of this leveling dragged the cultivated few down rather than uplifted the uncultivated, but it was optimistically predicted that this evil would be remedied in time. Even in its early stage of development during the antebellum period, travel and descriptive writers declared American society was improving at an amazing rate of speed. American commentators granted an angularity of manners here, but American rudeness, it was noted, grew out of the republican principle which held that individual consequence was completely a matter of opinion. A few commentators laid the blame for America's gilded vulgarity on the overriding concern for moneymaking and the deification of hard work, which were incompatible with the development of the finest society, but more often than not they also praised how social positions in America were not regulated by court precedence, entailed wealth, or ancestry—every American fought for his own castle of dignity, and an air of defiance was part of the American mien. An American must be careful not to let politeness imply deference or inferiority, and it is this cultural sentiment which Emerson touched when he spoke of manliness superseding form in the matter of social manners.

Travel and descriptive writers did not fail to note that

foreign critics derided American artistic and literary tastes as well as American social tastes. Commentators confessed a close relationship between the slow development of arts in the United States and the nation's practical needs, but in the mechanical arts they yielded to no nation. They predicted improvements in architectural taste, in the fine arts, and in the publication of magazines and reviews. In time, it was concluded, the demands of practicality and utility would be appeased, and Americans would then have time and money to cultivate literature and science. Further, it was felt that enough had been done to indicate America was not wanting in talent and learning. American travel and descriptive writers were eager—actually, they found it imperative—to convince Europe and their fellow Americans of America's coming of age culturally.

One typical rejoinder to the European travelers, who found a paucity of high culture here, was expressed by the creation of travels and descriptions of a mythic national character, a character based on simple and natural principles. This mythic character was juxtaposed to the effeteness of European manners, life, and culture. American manners were to harmonize with an individual's nature and character. This dedication to simplicity in the national character vis-à-vis European pomp expressed itself in many ways among American commentators. For instance, the American devotion to simplicity was said to extend to the grave; gorgeous tombs were unnecessary in the the republican country. The latter opinion represents the popular side of the Thoreauvian mind.

This Thoreauvian character in the popular mind is further revealed in the obvious pride travel and descriptive writers took in the fact that the president's mansion was elegant but not imposing. It was also a point of pride to be able to note that Philadelphia had no palaces. Palaces represented indications of pomp and vanity, negative values in an egalitarian society. American homes were described as embodying social comfort. Finally, travel and descriptive writers responded to foreign criticism by accepting the formless, fluctuating nature of the national character as a positive, not negative, feature. The American was encouraged to rejoice in his unpredictable, protean self. After all, the writers observed, American society was by its very nature and laws prevented from being fenced in or privileged. All comers had an equal chance. Usages did not take years to ripen and be carefully nurtured; they were tried, exhausted, dropped, and replaced as easily as one changes his clothes. Some commentators delighted to let the world know that Americans had no restrictive social opinions, no prejudices, and no habits.

The burden of this book is to show how, by probing the self-analysis antebellum Americans made in a representative group of popular travel and descriptive literature, one arrives at the matrices of our national character. My objective is to discuss what Americans said and believed about themselves and their civilization in their travel literature. Moreover, I will demonstrate in the course of anatomizing these collective self-portraits that mass culture states and transmits its beliefs about itself, tests its reality, and works out its identity in prosaic media. Although the historian has long been alert to the value of this class of books, he has generally used individual books in researching specific topics in American history. As a result, American books of travel and description have been studied more often on an individual basis rather than as a group of materials which might reveal recurrent cultural themes and patterns. However, in this book the culture's postures and indices of value are traced through content analysis of a travel and descriptive book grouping.

American travel and descriptive writing contains a mine of cultural information and presents the cultural historian with an opportunity to reconstruct the major parts of the national character as they developed in the early nineteenth century. The ideas explored and the interpretations made here are those which contribute new material for the reconstruction of antebellum culture's essential design. This reconstruction has yielded fairly precise, nonmathematical indices of national character which guide the cultural historian, the structural anthropologist, and students of American history to a fuller recognition of our culture. The indices and the configuration which resulted from a clustering of indices suggest that high and mass culture work from a common cultural design.

An understanding of the configuration which emerges in this book can best be made if at this point the materials used, the perspective from which they were studied, and the undergirding assumptions are described. One must start by examining the literary genre. Travels, oral and written, are an old form of literature, going back to the works of ancient Greek and Roman historians. It seems the most natural of human actions to leave one's homeland or village in order to learn more about the world and the strangers who inhabit the world beyond one's own living space. It is Renaissance travel literature which is the most important in putting the antebellum use of the genre into perspective.

America's earliest specimens of literature consist of accounts by travelers. This literature often falls into a gray area between the belletristic and the practical. It has creative aspects, including a utopian imaginative strain, an autobiographical stamp, and a historical character. What is significant, however, is the world view found in travel and descriptive literature. It did in fact serve as an important source of information about the world for Western culture, especially after the discovery of the New World, and it is connected to one of the most important movements of the Renaissance, the new science. There was a great thirst for knowledge of the physical world, and the royal societies of Europe encouraged explorers and travelers to record and collect information.

For much of their New World view, Europeans depended upon the traveler. The early travel book usually contained two parts. First, there was the narrative of the journey; second, there was the factual information collected in the course of traveling. In terms of the development of the travel book, as an art form, the placing of the practical information is important. Although the placement varied, the literary travel book eventually demoted prosaic information or incorporated it stylistically and thematically into its body. *Moby Dick* represents the outstanding example of the latter use. In the development of the genre, one finds practical and scientific information slowly moved into appendices and the narrative part of the journey placed at the forefront of the travel book. Of course, there were exceptions where writers skillfully blended both elements, the narrative of the journey and prosaic information, into a coherent and interesting unit.

The process by which especially seventeenth- and eighteenth-century travel and descriptive writing developed is important for understanding the turn which the genre took during the antebellum period. Early travels were written by explorers and adventurers who set out to achieve personal or national gain. Their motives for writing, as Professor Percy Adams has shown in *Travelers and Travel Liars* (1962), were economic, political, and egoistic. When travelers and explorers returned from their journeys, they satisfied a demand for information about the world by writing books. Travel accounts were very popular as a source of information, as entertainment, and as promotional literature. The last element contains the roots of American utopian writing and boosterism. Many travelers knew how to tell a good story. Exaggerations were common. A great deal was accepted and expected by readers. There were many travel liars, and their lies were influential in terms of intellectual history and had a long-lasting effect. There were unintentional mistakes, of course. Nevertheless, braggadocio types like John Smith contributed a sizable amount of literature which was to a considerable extent imaginative but was passed off as fact. As a result of these travels, the seventeenth and eighteenth centuries' world views were often askew, and by the end of the eighteenth century two traditions regarding travel and descriptive writing were accepted; first, travelers are untrustworthy; second, travelers' accounts are useful sources of knowledge. However, it might be noted, the tone of early American travel and descriptive literature was zesty, full of the promise of endless plenty, and full of accounts of human satisfaction with this new world. This tone existed despite the fearsome Indians and the ruthless wilderness. The ruthless land helped shape an aggressive American character, and the utopian hope of early American travels persisted and joined that aggressiveness to form the essential national character. In the nineteenth century, faster methods of transportation and communications and the powerful effect of empirical science made much more accurate observations and reporting inevitable.

In her unpublished dissertation "Early Development in America, 1825–1850, of Travel Books as Literature," Ann L. Greer categorizes the various types of antebellum travel books and concludes that a unified, coherent modern travel book developed in the period; however, in considering the genre broadly, as I have done for this study, it is difficult to see any widespread coherence developing in the genre, and the genre remained throughout the period very flexible and often amorphous. Twentieth-century students of the travel book have defined it as an account of a trip actually taken by the writer, written some time soon after the trip, having as its objective entertainment and instruction. (Greer emphasizes entertainment over instruction.) Commentators on the genre have looked at it from the literary standpoint generally, but this study, of course, concerns itself with the genre as a cultural tool.

I grant at the very beginning that the genre involves a potage of elements and encompasses wide diversity. The idea of travel or movement from a place known to another unknown is the crux of the genre. We find discursive commentary on subjects as diversified as women's rights and a visitor's response to Natural Bridge in Virginia. The formal essay interrupts the travel and descriptive narrative as naturally as does the inclusion of such practical information as the listing of good hotels. Folklore, anecdotes, poetry, sermons—all sorts of literary and subliterary elements—intrude into the travel and descriptive books, in some books gracefully, in others awkwardly. Using a fictional framework loosely is not unusual for the travel or descriptive book, but of course once that framework is surmounted by greater fictional purposes of the writer, the book can no longer be considered a travel or descriptive book. Thus, the travel and descriptive books studied here more often than not have a hodgepodge character, although they are not incoherent stylistically. I have used the artful book as well as the journalistic book. Both types have reportorial and autobiographical elements which maintain for their readers an aura of travel literature. Most of the books supplying the material for the conclusions made here have not used the reportorial or autobiographical element of travel literature for artistic purposes, but have tried to do something a little below that to which we generally accord the term "belletristic." These distinctions lead me to observe that the great masterpieces of American literature in the nineteenth century are more related to the prosaic travel and descriptive writings around which I center my attention in this book than they are to the novel. As we move toward the final chapter, the reason for this relationship will be clearer, and what the mass audience read will be discussed with the travels of A. Gordon Pym, Tommo-Ishmael-Redburn-Melville, Richard Henry Dana, and Huck Finn in mind.

The richness of the mass of travel and descriptive books for the study of the national character becomes further apparent when one probes the elements of which the books chosen for this study are composed. Four types have been used here; the "literary," that is, the more artful and traditional travel book; the sketchbook-like general descriptive book; the prosaic guidebook; and the broadly organized, often encyclopedic gazetteer. The literary travel book has an immediate and personal tone, because there is in it a heavy emphasis on the writer's character and the delineation of a clearly defined trip. The general descriptive book resembles the literary kind of book, although it contains less emphasis on a precisely defined and chronologically arranged trip. In the guidebook and the gazetteer, the character of the writer or editor becomes less apparent and the perspective of the book is very broad and usually impersonal. Nevertheless, these four types of books share similar substantive and stylistic elements. The major element of travel, taking a trip, preparing someone else for a trip, or researching a book by traveling, links them to one another; they have the similar concerns of the explorer-describer and travel narrator. In addition to the latter characteristic, all four types of books interborrowed materials, influenced each other by interborrowing, and used as source material standard popular books published earlier. It is important not to lose sight of the latter point, because it makes possible finding something coherent to say about the culture through a grouping of the books.

The development of the travel and descriptive book in this period can be better understood when one considers that Thomas Addison Richards' *American Scenery* (1854) and John Pendleton Kennedy's *Swallow Barn* (1832), for instance, make use of weak fictional frameworks to include the essentials of travel and descriptive writing. Kennedy in a preface to the 1851 edition of his book instructed his readers that his book was not a novel. He had planned it as a series of sketches connected by the methods of the travel writer; it was to have the character of a travel book, a diary, a collection of letters, a drama, and a history. One can look at the structure and accomplishment of Thoreau's *A Week on the Concord and Merrimack Rivers* (1849) with this popular usage and understanding of the genre in mind. James Russell Lowell's review of Thoreau's book chides Thoreau's digressions and cries for more Merrimacking; however, Lowell's judgment was colored more by personal animosities than by a lack of understanding of the flexibility of the genre. Lowell demonstrated a clear understanding of the genre in his "Moosehead Journal." The fact that Kennedy made the emphasis mentioned above is testimony to the popularity of the travel and descriptive book genre and to what the antebellum audience expected of it. In fact, Kennedy's book is not a travel book in many respects. Richards' book, despite its fictional framework, remains essentially travel description. The distinction in the matter of the genre rests on the force of the individual writer's imagination. In a man like Thoreau the force surmounts the travel book genre and leads him to say something highly personal and rich about reality. When Melville triumphs in *Redburn, Moby Dick,* and *The Confidence-Man,* all the elements of the genre bend to his will and integrity.

The lines of the travel book genre were often broadly drawn, resulting in much overlapping among several types of books. As a result of this overlapping, some of the books seem to fall into more than one of the four classes described above. It is not surprising that the books have a potpourri character when one considers the standard held for them by mass antebellum culture and expressed by Henry T. Tuckerman in his antebellum survey of American travel and descriptive writing. Tuckerman maintained that the travel and descriptive book writer who wanted a true knowledge of the country had to go beyond a casual study of its external features and encompass the country's character, its history, its romance, its art, and its poetry.

Literary travel book and general descriptive book writers tried to measure up to a standard of catholicity in subject matter and style. In addition to the occasional information on the quality of hotels, on train fares, travel distances, etc., some authors supplied fishing lore and hunting information, adventure tales, humorous anecdotes, legends and folklore, and original poetry. Prophetic observations and political propaganda are found in these books also. Caroline Gilman included in *The Poetry of Travelling in the United States* (1838) history, poetry, legends, and social commentary; Frederick Law Olmsted in *A Journey in the Seaboard Slave States* (1856) described rice planting, turpentine making, and sugar cane growing; in Bayard Taylor's *Eldorado* (1850) the antebellum reader received a firsthand account of the California Constitutional Convention, a general description of westering, and a history of the California missions; Henry Ward Beecher's *Star Papers* (1855) portrayed his summer rambles—a visit to Jonathan Edward's house in Stockbridge, Massachusetts, and an enthusiastic essay on elm trees; William Cullen Bryant in *Letters of a Traveller* (1851) recorded accounts of folk medicine and included cautionary remarks to immigrants; and Lewis H. Garrand in *Wah-to-Yah and the Taos Trail* (1850) gave his readers a tall tale about a trip to Hell.

The antebellum guidebook and gazetteer tended to be directed to the practical needs of Americans than did the literary travel book and the general descriptive book. The guidebook and gazetteer satisfied requests for bald, factual travel information. In the typical guidebook and gazetteer, the antebellum American found information regarding fares, routes, and travel dangers emphasized; tours were outlined; tourists going to the city or into the country were told the response such experiences called for; and endless statistics on the cost of buildings, assets of businesses, sizes of towns, etc., were faithfully presented. The presentation of this prosaic information was not without significance, however. Furthermore, guidebook and gazetteer writers included in their books legends, anecdotes, and travel incidents, which were culled from their personal experience or that of others. Thumbnail sketches of historical sites, comments on educational and benevolent institutions, and descriptions of museums, newspapers, and factories were recorded in gazetteers. In the so-called emigrant guidebook the prospective emigrant found directions to the West and propagandistic descriptions of what he would find there, but in these guidebooks myths, tall tales, and folklore were chronicled also.

Many writers of the four types of travel and descriptive books supplemented their own travel experience with the unpublished and published experiences of others—sometimes acknowledging their debt and at other times not doing so. There was a reliance on communications from friends and acquaintances for information about areas which writers described but in which they had not traveled. Popular geographies and almanacs, local and general histories, and European and American scientific works were used. Jedidiah Morse, Benjamin Silliman, Sir Charles Lyell, Louis Agassiz, John J. Audubon, and Alexander Wilson were popular authorities. Older out-of-date travel guides and city handbooks were called upon to supply information for new guides. One finds references to Thomas Jefferson's *Notes on the State of Virginia,* the work of Cadwallader Colden, Jonathan Carver, John Heckewelder, and other American writing. Much American and English prose and poetry was quoted, often with a studied preference for native writers; Cooper was frequently used. The accounts of foreign travelers who gave favorable reports about the United States received attention. Because there was substantial interborrowing among contemporary books of travel and description and the use of similar allusions among them, the books had a commonality, and thus shared a remarkable coherent body of common cultural resources. This fact helps make clear how the books were transmitters of cultural values.

The writers of travel and descriptive books usually claimed some firsthand experience and observation for their works. Sixteen thousand miles of travel went into the preparation of Barber and Howe's *Our Whole Country,* a general descriptive book. E. S. Seymour wrote his emigrant guide in the West which he described. Charles Lanman's *Adventure in the Wilds of the United States* (1859) contained the results of summer trips throughout the country during a period of ten years. Frederick Law Olmsted traveled extensively in the course of preparing his books about the South. John Hayward claimed a considerable amount of travel was required to write *A Gazetteer of the United States* (1853). Starr King's many trips to New Hampshire resulted in his popular book about the White Mountains. Wellington Williams asserted that his *Appleton's Northern and Eastern Traveller's Guide* (1852) contained much material acquired from actual observation.

Travel and descriptive writers had varied motives for traveling in and writing about their native land. Some writers moved about their country plainly for pleasure and relaxation. Frederick Law Olmsted maintained that he wrote in order to describe what he had found interesting, amusing, and instructive in his travels, although in saying so he underplayed his serious interest in southern culture and slavery. Other writers sought health and adventure in travel. For instance, George Wilkins Kendall went west in search of health, the primitive wilderness, writing materials, and the sport and adventure of life there. It is surprising to find a goodly number of antebellum Americans undergoing arduous journeys for their health! The more prosaic writers of guides and gazetteers wanted to inform their readers and give them an accurate conception of places. The emigrant guidebook boosted the West, while other books clearly courted the fireside traveler.

Charles Lanman's travel book was a sort of encyclopedia of American scenery, personal adventures, and traveling anecdotes intended to reveal the manners and customs of Americans and to interest nauralists and sportsmen. Through his *American Scenery* (1854) Thomas Addison Richards hoped to foster landscape appreciation and the art of the landscape artist. Joel Headley wanted to make the primitive Adirondacks better known through his travel book. Because he assumed tourists spent their money and time not to sample White Mountain gastronomy, Starr King intended through his descriptive book to help people appreciate landscape more fully.

Horace Greeley traveled and wrote to get and give first-hand information about the West. Others wanted to make known curious and changing aspects of American society, to instruct and entertain readers, to increase good will between different sections of the country, and to sketch manners, customs, and natural and artistic curiosities. Some writers claimed grandiosely that they had written homebooks and heirlooms for every American family. Travel and descriptive writers aspired to write for all classes; many wanted to give a grand survey of the Republic. There was a strong inclination among writers of all four classes of books to illustrate the prosperity, the glory, and the admiration of the world which, for them, American civilization had become.

Given this mixture of motives for writing and the complexity of the travel book genre, an attempt to uncover fundamental patterns of culture from a content analysis of travel and descriptive books required criteria for choosing the books which would promise as much accuracy as possible in a cultural history. It was necessary to include books from each decade of the period, although because of interborrowing and the long use of books written in the early nineteenth century, books written in the forties and fifties contained patterns which were more surely developed in the antebellum period. Books were chosen which were popular during the period, ones having a broad readership and a wide distribution, for example, books first published in newspapers, published in cheap editions, and written by popular travelers. As much as possible, books written by antebellum Americans with differing or broad sectional outlooks were given special priority. Henry T. Tuckerman's pioneering study of American travel and descriptive literature helped in the selection and elimination of many writers because his book capitalized on the antebellum interest in travel and descriptive literature. The reading of a great many books and the collation of ideas and patterns helped determine subsequent additions to the group of books used in my content analysis.

The dangers of grouping a selection of books and having them say something about a culture were kept clearly before the writer. I carefully avoided trying to impose a form upon the books which might be preconceived, fully realizing the risk of subjectivity this kind of study assumes. There are areas of imprecision in cultural studies, less inevitable in scientific studies, but the opportunity of trying to make clearer how a culture works through its prosaic and literary materials, how it communicates and tries to work out its problems, seemed to make the risks worthwhile. However, elemental principles of scientific study were applied to my choices. Initially, lists of writers quoted in travel and descriptive books and recurrent ideas were scrutinized in terms of the frequency of their appearance, and an attempt was made to predict the appearance and structuring of culturing patterns in other books. Differences in intellectual background, differences of reactions and reporting because of age, sex, and regional base

found among the writers studied played a part in the selection
and rejection of materials. Differences of opinions were noted
in terms of how they affected the major statements which this
book makes in identifying the essential elements in the culture, and taken into account as I formulated my conclusions.
Also, in choosing books for inclusion in this study, I kept an
eye on the foreign travelers of the period, and considered
remarks they made about American culture in general, about
antebellum travel, and about the way the American mind approached itself symbolically or unconsciously.

It must be admitted that at the beginning of this study I
had to go it blind, but it was not long before the backwashes
of travel and descriptive books gave hints of values, beliefs,
and patterns of culture waiting to be uncovered, and these
hints yielded a national configuration vital and significant in
terms of understanding what cultural motivation accounts for
the behavior of Americans and their attempts to understand
and appraise themselves.

During the antebellum period, when Americans still
smarted from the antagonistic 1821 questions of Sydney Smith
which underlined the nakedness of culture in America, when
Americans were angered at the descriptions of their culture
by British travelers like Mrs. Trollope, Basil Hall, and
Charles Dickens, and when they were being told that they had
"listened too long to the courtly muses of Europe," travel
and descriptive writers took part in trying to understand the
true life and nature of America and to learn what was unique
about their land and the life of Americans. The work of these
writers helped to suggest outlines of the national character
which writers greater than they could transform into more
poetic and lasting expressions. These writers subtly worked
out and transmitted the keynotes of American culture.

2

THE DELIGHT OF TRAVEL

A keynote of American culture has been activism, and
the factor that made possible the mass popularity of travel
and descriptive books was the antebellum transportation revolution. Joined to American activism, this revolution fostered
a substantial development of pleasure travel; playing the role
of the tourist became an American fad. The history of this
fad is briskly recorded by travel and descriptive writers. When
we seek to uncover the cultural meanings hidden in the backwashes of travel and descriptive writing, we find the starting
point is the study of what the writers said about the atmosphere of American travel and of the pleasure travel interests
of antebellum Americans.

Travels, descriptive books, guides, and gazetteers willingly stepped forward to serve the flourishing group of Americans who wanted to use their new internal improvements in
the northern and middle Atlantic states to tour the country.
Travel writers made it known that it was now possible for
Americans to make trips which fifty years before had been
long and tedious, usually in wagons or on horseback. The
antebellum period was declared the era of traveling, and
Americans were called a wandering people. Masses, it was
written, thronged public travel conveyances for improvement

and pleasure. Crowds of tourists and their habits awaited description. Traveling was acknowledged to be an American habit rather than an event. The tone of travel and descriptive writers in describing their fellow Americans pursuing pleasure travel was feverish, and by proclaiming a great frenzy of movement within American society, the writers of travels satisfied, as well as expressed, unconsciously the American thirst for movement and for search as an appropriate means of discovering reality and self. Thus, Starr King bragged that by 1849 not less than five thousand people made the climb up Mount Washington every summer by the regular bridle path, and forty thousand yearly visitors to Niagara were heralded as evidencing how enthusiastic a tourist the American had become.

Americans were exhorted by travel writers to go somewhere, anywhere, if they could. Purportedly, steamers leaving the city were crowded with tourists in the summer. Americans were described in travel and descriptive books as rushing in masses to watering places, to the falls, to the seashore, to lakes and mountains, and to natural curiosities or wonders, and Caroline Gilman called the American propensity for travel a mania. Whether the writers of descriptive books were reporting faithfully what they saw and, therefore, were giving readers a picture of actual American tourist activities, or whether they attempted to stimulate the tourist industry through their books is not as important as the fact that these descriptions were widely read and represent what Americans wanted or came to believe about themselves.

Although a sudden increase in pleasure travel brought an unpleasant crowding of facilities, antebellum tourists rushed to enjoy the excitement of steamboat, canal boat, or railroad travel. Steamboat activities included races between steamers, shooting animals from the boat, the hawking of sundry goods by peddlers, drinking and gaming, and ubiquitous conversations in which topics ranged from the price of horses to the value of a slave. The social mood of steamboat travel was put to excellent artistic advantage by Melville in *The Confidence-*

Man (1857). On a canal boat travelers were told to be wary
of decapitation by low bridges, and the speed of railroads
frightened and exhilarated tourists.

Although *Our Summer Retreats* in 1858 catalogues 14
major areas of antebellum pleasure travels and 112 secondary
places of popular resort, the former including the Catskills,
Niagara Falls, the Virginia springs, and the White Mountains,
the latter including resort areas in Maine, Nebraska, the Gulf
of Mexico, and Minnesota, the listings are misleading; it
should be emphasized that the East supported the great bulk
of pleasure traveling described by antebellum writers. The
South and the West had a few small resorts. Nevertheless, such
listings are suggestive of what was happening on the pleasure
travel scene and what Americans hoped for. Pleasure travel
comes alive in the travel vignettes given to us by the writers.
Describing the pleasure of a short trip, William Cullen Bryant
in 1847 traveled through New England by railroad, and at
Durham, New Hampshire, and shortly after at Dover, New
Hampshire, he saw two trainloads of noisy and smiling Sunday
school children about to start out on a picnic party in Maine.
Bryant later passed by an oak grove in which long tables and
benches awaited the picnickers as his train preceded theirs
into Maine. At nine o'clock in the evening Charles Fenno
Hoffman rushed to board a Cleveland steamboat going west.
It was 1833 and the quay was in great confusion; the night
was dark and dusty, lit only by single lanterns moving to and
fro, the boat and wharf were crowded with boxes and the
belongings of emigrants, and the air was filled with a Babel-
like screaming, orders and countermands, and the harsh
hissing of steam.

The widely distributed Appleton guidebooks outlined
tours up the Hudson, to Niagara, to the White Mountains,
to western cities, to Mammoth Cave, and summer excursions
from New York to Chicago. If a traveler had only a few days,
a trip to the Long Island or the New Jersey shore or up the
Hudson was deemed pleasant by travel writers. On a tour up
the Hudson, the traveler could look forward to the enjoyment

of the scenery, visits to West Point, Newburgh, or the Catskills; and perhaps an excursion to Lake George or Fort
Ticonderoga might be added to his itinerary. The pleasure
traveler was given a tour of the White Mountains to consider,
or he might spend three weeks visiting the wonder and
admiration of the world, Niagara Falls. A four weeks excursion might include the Virginia springs via Philadelphia,
Baltimore, and Washington; and once the tourist reached
Virginia, side trips to Natural Bridge, Weir's Cave, and the
Peaks of Otter were to be seriously considered. With enough
time, he might proceed from Virginia to Mammoth Cave in
Kentucky, which was considered a natural curiosity second
only to Niagara in grandeur. For the male traveler, a hunting
expedition in the wild fastnesses of the Adirondacks was
proposed.

The watering place was described as the focal point of
pleasure travel in the period, probably drawing the largest
number of tourists. The reasons for visiting the watering place
reveal much about the national character. Saratoga, for instance, was a place to rest in the midst of American hurry; at
Harrodsburg Springs, Kentucky, the tourist could escape the
world of competition. One could escape the summer heat of
the city at the Virginia springs. Travel writers tell about
American tourists who went to their watering places to take
the waters, to escape the city, to hunt scenery, and to find
relaxation in outdoor and social activities.

The mineral waters at the spas were great panaceas for
all illnesses known to man. Travel writers touted the healthful
benefits to be found in the waters when combined with fresh
air, rural scenery, exercise in the course of exciting excursions,
pleasant society, and complete rest from business activities.
Americans were assured that they could relax and enjoy their
summer trip without guilt, but as if this assurance were not
sufficient, they were asked to consider that relaxation was
practical. A visit to the spa was a necessary renewal of one's
health in order to carry on with the activities of life during
the remainder of the year. As a result, travel and descriptive

writers spent much time giving their readers chemical break-downs of the waters, testimonials of doctors and professors regarding their beneficial aspects, the differences among the several mineral springs, and telling them that social life at the spa would renovate the juices which had been exhausted in making money. Some travel and descriptive writers were wary of the use of mineral waters and saw an overemphasis on the waters' curative powers as a dangerous subterfuge for enjoying a summer vacation and making new social acquaintances. Despite the ridicule and criticism, a good number of tourists no doubt followed the regimen of drinking and bathing in the mineral waters. Some guidebook writers knew that in the fluctuating social world of American culture, Americans were eager to know exactly how to behave.

Tourists were told they might drink four to eight glasses of mineral water. In the event this amount caused an unpleas-ant sensation, the tourist was advised to discontinue using the waters. It was suggested that the tourist arise about six o'clock and immediately go to the spring to take a small glass of water. Next, a brisk walk was in order. Another drink of water at six-thirty and moderate exercise thereafter until seven was recommended. Breakfast at eight o'clock was to be moderate and of a suitable quality—a nice, tender mutton chop, or a soft-boiled egg (the egg was to be fresh and not preserved in lime), or venison, or beefsteak. After breakfast a drive, ride, or general amusement was prescribed; the tourist was to amuse himself in social intercourse or gentle exercise until supper, which might consist of black tea or a glass of milk and a cracker. Dancing was permissible in the evening, but in moderation and only until ten o'clock, when the tourist should retire to his room, avoiding the gaming room as he would death and Hell.

The latter dour statement from an Appleton guidebook cannot be accepted as a typical description of what pleasure tourists did in fact have at their mineral spas. Other books describe mineral water bathing as a refreshing and enjoyable occupation; once again, the regimen for bathing in the minerals is exactly described, but with more concern for practicality and for imparting useful information. Life at Saratoga and other springs was described by travel writers as including dancing, dressing elegantly, and flirting. Some writers described the springs as places of frivolity, superficiality, and high living. Joel Headley poked fun at tourists, who speaking of going into the country, meant going to the comfortable amenities of Saratoga, Nahant, and New Rochelle. Social life without doubt was the keynote at most spas, and smoking, chatting about stocks, and the social whirl were major amusements. After all, writers understood one went to the spa to see new people and make new acquaintances. The northern spa might see two or three arrivals a week, and life was described as fashionable and a continual festival.

Specific amusements which travel writers held out to spa visitors included bowling, billiards, concerts, walking, railroad excursions, reading, awaiting the arrival of other tourists, talking about manners, gossiping, and dancing. One might take a mountain tramp with a flask of brandy slung over one's shoulder for a picturesque effect. Congress Hall at Saratoga held five hundred guests in the evening. On ball night, a group of black musicians, placed on a dining room table, played "Hail, Columbia!"; the well-dressed guests marched in, led by the patroness and a prominent wealthy man. Then the dancing began, young men and women walked outdoors on the colonnade, and at eleven champagne went around for the ladies while the gentlemen took something stronger at the bar. Thereafter, everyone was brighter and more agreeable.

As the antebellum period progressed, the seashore resorts competed with the watering place for a share of the tourist trade. Newport's popularity grew in the opinion of travel and descriptive writers to the highest point as a fashionable resort. In fact, among some writers it gained the reputation, sometimes attributed to Saratoga and other watering places, of having a feverish and unrestful social atmosphere. The tourist was cautioned by some writers to seek out quiet country towns for summer pleasure travel. Newport was attacked as encouraging, again as Saratoga purportedly did, false responses to nature and a frenzied search for continual amusement. Despite this criticism, Newport was admired by many writers for its fashionable dress, the din of dancing music, scandal, flirtation, and ocean serenades. There was a crush of activity, and one concludes from reading travel writers that antebellum Americans approached their summer pleasures less with a need for relaxation and quiet than for social activity and movement, however much they wanted to believe there was incessant dawdling and lounging at resorts. There were sailing, riding, and races on Newport's hard, black beach. Along the open Atlantic the best beaches served antebellum Americans in the summer similarly, although on a lower key. In this age the summer vacation became available to the common man. Cape May was valued as a resort for tired Americans; its beach was rated unsurpassed for bathing, and daily boats left from Philadelphia to Cape May in summer. The fare was three dollars. Long Branch was popular also, and one learns from travel writers that dozens of smaller and more isolated beaches served the pleasure traveler from 1830 to 1861. Toward the end of the era Maine's Mount Desert Island became a popular resort for artists and summer loungers.

Early in the period tourist life at American lakes had a more tranquil tone than it did at Saratoga and Newport, but eventually complaints of the hurrying American tourist at the lakes began to appear also. Lake George in New York and Lake Winnepesaukee in New Hampshire attracted tourists who hiked, bowled, sat on a piazza, fished, and sailed. Some went to find the respite from city life not available at the spas. Mountain resorts in the Catskills and the White Mountains were extensively visited during the antebellum period. The Catskill Mountain House offered one of the most popularized views among the resorts and was considered very fashionable. The hotel stood on the edge of a cliff, and the tourist was promised a view which extended from Long Island Sound to the White Mountains. Twice a day during the summer, stages brought summer loungers to enjoy that view and eat such delicacies as charlotte russe. Formal wear at dinner was not expected but was no doubt common, and tourists had to be warned to wear cowhide boots, not varnished pumps, while hiking to the nearby falls. As the White Mountains attracted more visitors in the era, a variety of resort luxuries became available there. Tourists visited the notches, the flume, and crowned their trip perhaps with an ascent of Mount Washington.

Descriptions of lofty prospects in travel and descriptive writing enticed the tourists to the mountain resorts. Wellington Williams in his *Northern and Eastern* Appleton guidebook quoted a Reverend J.S.C. Abbot's "Ascent of Mount Washington" for his readers. In Abbot's account a party of thirteen, three women and ten men including a guide, traveled to the summit of Mount Washington on horseback, each with a knapsack filled with picnic provisions. The guests at the inn who were to stay behind assembled to send the cavalcade off with enthusiasm. On the way the party passed the time joking, and singing. At the end of a six-mile ride, the difficult ascent began, and upon arriving at the summit, the party spread their refreshments on a flat rock and picnicked. By 1855 the Tip Top House with its deck-roof and telescope had been erected for the enjoyment of summer visitors.

The famous natural wonders of the country, Natural Bridge of Virginia, Mammoth Cave in Kentucky, and Niagara Falls in New York, were high on the popularity lists of tourist attractions described by travel writers. Visitors who went to the Virginia springs invariably took in Natural Bridge, and tourists were guided through the romantically named chambers of Mammoth Cave by the mulatto guide Stephen. In the summer Sunday religious services were held in the cave. Niagara, however, was first and foremost in terms of popularity with pleasure travelers. Thousands of travelers yearly went to see what was described by travel writers as one of the wonders of the world. Very early Niagara became a busy tourist spot; Indian curiosities, canes, and refreshments were available at various gift shops. Dressed in green Indian-rubber outfits for an excursion by water to the falls, visitors were said to experience the driving, sweeping, thundering cataract exuberantly. They were impressed as the falls crammed the air with sound. Travel and descriptive writers made of this tourist experience a religio-cultural event. On clear moonlight evenings the local army band often assembled on the banks of the river near the falls and blended its stirring, martial sounds with the grand diapason of Niagara's thundering hymn. According to *Pecks' Tourist Companion,* tourists were enraptured by hearing the anthems of nature accompanied by men.

The fast-paced lifestyle antebellum Americans claimed for themselves in their travel and descriptive books is emphatically presented in descriptions of tourist activities in large cities. Writers described the growth of American cities as very rapid, and the character of city life and its amusements suggested an atmosphere of bustle and excitement. The typical tourist itinerary described by travel writers records what Americans put on their lists of things to see and do in the city; the national character, as at the resorts, was restless and eager to keep moving, growing and assessing itself materially. New York within the framework of the developing national self-consciousness became din, hurry, and intense anxiety. It was characterized as Broadway and broiled oysters; and on Broadway stood Stewart's Marble Palace, the world's most extensive and fashionable shopping place for ladies. The tourist was told to note that Stewart's employed three hundred fifty clerks and sold several million dollars worth of dry goods annually. Ball, Black and Company and Tiffany and Company sold jewelry and silverware, Tiffany retailing up to one million dollars annually.

Boston was considered more sober and substantial in contrast to the livelier New York. Boston fell behind the times and closed its shops at dark, while at New York and Philadelphia as much business was done after dark as in the daytime, giving, according to travel writers, New York and Philadelphia a youthful and gay tone. Although Boston may have been considered more staid, representing granite respectability, its elegant Common was often crowded with tourists on holidays. Baltimore also had its promenade and fashionable quarter which were said to exude wealth and prosperity. Most books, with typical antebellum braggadocio and a sense of insecurity, proclaimed Washington the equal of any capital in the world. Its slow growth was often acknowledged, but government buildings and the magnificent plan of the city were a source of pride among travel writers. The tourist could relish the fact that his capital was built on a magnificent scheme; its location insured the success of the scheme; its easy access to the sea gave it every chance for commercial greatness; and its topography made for a picturesque and beautiful city. Theodore Dwight, Jr., saw its slow growth as an advantage because political intrigues were less likely when a large metropolis and its population do not conceal intrigues from view. Washington's society was dubbed an every-body-dom society, because of its egalitarian tone, and it is interesting to find Caroline Gilman believing a visit to the capital city imperfect without an introduction to the president.

Travel and descriptive writers discovered a feeling of antiquity and grace in Charleston, South Carolina; these characteristics were considered residues of the colonial period. The two most famous attractions of Charleston were the races and the February balls. Travel writers described the tone of New Orleans as European. According to Nathaniel Parker Willis, New Orleans was the Paris of Western gay life, studded with temples of drink, pervaded by a come-take-a-drink attitude, and featuring slave auctions where luncheon tables set for the pleasure of visitors graced the auction room. New Orleans amusements were the theater, the circus, tenpin alley, billiards, cafes, saloons, and gaming at the gambling halls. The raw city of San Francisco in 1850 had a startling aspect at night. According to Bayard Taylor, the mostly canvas houses were made transparent by lamps inside, and points of light shone more brilliantly where the decoy lamps of gaming houses were set out. From the gaming houses came by fits the sound of music, muffled by street sounds. San Francisco had an unreal and fantastic aura which seemed to Taylor like that of a magic-lantern city capable of being built or annihilated by the motion of the hand. The latter statement contains a symbol of the antebellum American's uncertainty about himself and the world he was creating.

America assuaged its uncertainty by shouting its own self-approval, somewhat as a child whistles in the dark. As a result, travel and descriptive writers scrupulously gave an accounting of the civilized amenities and luxuries awaiting the tourist in the large cities. For example, the St. Nicolas Hotel in New York spent forty thousand dollars for mirrors and fifty thousand dollars for silverware and Sheffield plate. As it began to do all sorts of tasks in the city, the steam engine was singled out as a symbol of progress and comfort in America. Travel writers assured tourists through this information that the United States was becoming a mature and wealthy civilization; thus, steam machines were approached by tourists with wonder and admiration.

Travel and descriptive writers devoted numerous pages to describing the high quality of American city accommodations. New York, called the emporium of the United States, boasted of Holt's Hotel. In 1833 Holt's offered, according to Gideon Miner Davison, a six-story white marble building, with a pleasant and spacious rotunda on its roof from which visitors could see nearly the whole city. Steam-driven machinery carried food to the guests. The second floor had drawing and sitting rooms, well lighted by many windows and elegantly furnished; the third floor contained parlor, dining, retiring, and receiving rooms for the use of married couples and families. A steam engine raised dumbwaiters from the basement to the tower, and by using forcing pumps each story had at all times cold and hot water for baths in the attic and for ordinary uses in other rooms.

Another example of this buttressing of the national ego by travel writers is seen in the encouragement of the city tourist to visit commercial, industrial, and civic institutions. Descriptions of visits to the Lowell factory system were common. Pittsburgh's glass and iron works were part of tourist itineraries. Philadelphia proudly opened its steam-operated sugar refinery to travelers. Travel and descriptive writers gave in their works extensive lists and descriptions of small and large city factories and instructions for interesting visits to them; also, visits to banks and other commercial establishments were recommended. The national character's insecurity regarding its material progress was assuaged by these trips taken by loyal citizens; however, the material side of civilization was not the only one emphasized by travel writers.

Tours of government and educational institutions were an important part of the tourist's city visit. Civic architecture was described and praised; a tour of a city usually included visiting popular local landmarks. Henry S. Tanner in his *The American Traveller* led the pleasure traveler in Baltimore to the following attractions: Washington Monument at Charles and Monument streets, where there was a colossal statue of Washington on a 163-foot pedestal, the battle monument in Calvert Street, the city spring in Calvert Street, the customs house, two colleges, university buildings, the courthouse, and the water works.

Visits to benevolent institutions were also high points described by travel writers for city tourists. These institutions included hospitals, schools for the blind, etc. In addition to having significance in terms of shoring an insecure national character, the encouragement given to tourists by travel writers to visit benevolent institutions is symptomatic of an antebellum eagerness to meet some of the foreign criticism regarding the quality of American humanitarian institutions. The visits no doubt gave cultural assurance to Americans that their country was not backward regarding humanitarianism and that it was on a par with European advances. Thus, many antebellum tourists were instructed by travel and descriptive writers to faithfully tour prisons, asylums, hospitals, poorhouses, etc., deriving cultural comfort for their efforts.

Not to be neglected were the important historical sites in the vicinity of American cities. Every traveler to Washington was expected to make a pilgrimage to Mount Vernon to view the remains of Washington, because this spot was deemed sacred to the mind of every American. A special steamboat went directly to Mount Vernon, and Caroline Gilman described sailing down the Potomac on the *Columbia* and shedding tears at the sight of Mount Vernon and the thought of Washington. Revolutionary and other historical shrines in the city environs had to be reverently visited, and heroes were to be properly worshiped. Through the material prosperity, humanitarian progress, and historical lore discovered in the city places to which tourists were sent by travel writers, the national character stored up assets for its reality and its self.

After performing the prescribed patriotic ritual visits, antebellum tourists had to be led to amusements and pleasures of a different sort. The city contained natural, artistic, and scientific curiosities to delight the traveler. Philadelphia had Barnum's museum, the "Chinese Saloon" with its curiosities, and Signor Blitz's feats of legerdemain in the Philadelphia Museum building. Baltimore had its museum of curiosities also, and in Washington the Smithsonian attracted tourists. New York offered the tourist in 1849 a display of the entire city in miniature—a perfect facsimile carved in wood containing two hundred thousand buildings which took 150 men and cost thirty thousand dollars to build. This New York curiosity covered an area of six hundred square feet, and it was displayed at 360 Broadway before it was to begin a national tour.

Baltimore and Cleveland had circuses. Elsewhere there were concerts, balls, lectures, singing schools, and theaters. Winter travelers to Philadelphia joined thousands roasting an ox on the ice and coasting on the snow. New York offered Wistar parties, scenic exhibitions and panoramas, an opera company, public gardens, fireworks, horse and boat racing, and skating. Late in the antebellum period the large pond in Central Park became a popular winter resort for skaters. On Christmas Day in 1859 fifty thousand people visited the park, eight thousand skated on the pond at one time, and as many looked on. When policemen feared the ice would give way under the crowd as the weather warmed, forty of them tried to drive off eight thousand skaters, but they failed.

The short excursion and promenade frequently demanded the attention of travel writers. As a matter of course, tourists in Baltimore were expected to ride to Elicott's mills, thirteen miles from the city. On the way the tourist was told he would see picturesque scenery, the Carrolton viaduct, and a bridge which was proclaimed a magnificent specimen of American architecture. Train excursions were popular too and were organized in many cities on special occasions. In Philadelphia a visit to the water works was highly esteemed. Romantic Schuylkill excursions included Fairmont, Laurel Hill cemetery, Schuylkill Falls, and Manayunk. Every hour through the day tourists were told they could have the pleasure of this trip for ten cents. The variety of scenery, the bridges, two water works, a canal, and the sight of trains were touted as attractions by travel and descriptive writers.

The Croton aqueduct enjoyed a great popularity among travelers. There was an ecstatic response to the aqueduct fountains which threw a column of water sixty feet into the air. Shifting the plate in the conduit pipe made the water take on different shapes: The Maid of the Mist, the Croton Plume, the Vase, the Dome, the Bouquet, the Sheaf of Wheat, and the Weeping Willow. The aqueduct was admired as a great feat of engineering, and the reservoir at Murray Hill, which was part of the system, was built in the Egyptian style with massive buttresses and crowned by an enclosed promenade. In New York the travel writer also recommended a ride to Fort Hamilton, or a ferryboat trip in the fog, or a ramble in Central Park, or a visit to Coney Island, or simply a promenade on Broadway. Castle Garden had a promenade and fireworks. No doubt smaller cities took advantage of their local nature spots in similar ways, and in the process the national character developed patterns of amusement. In central Massachusetts, for instance, visitors to Holyoke and Springfield might travel to the top of Mount Holyoke to see the magnificent views of the Connecticut River valley. A shanty and refreshments were available on the mountaintop.

The rural cemeteries, which developed in the 1830s outside large cities, were the focal point for many travel descriptions. The most famous rural cemeteries of the period were Mount Auburn in Massachusetts, Greenwood in New York, Laurel Hill in Philadelphia, Green Mount in Baltimore, and Magnolia in Charleston. The popularity of the rural or scenic cemetery spread rapidly in the era, and we find counterparts of Mount Auburn and Greenwood in smaller cities like Cincinnati, Savannah, Chicago, and Bangor, Maine. Separate guides were dedicated to the stranger and traveler visiting the cemeteries, including a series entitled *Rural Cemeteries of America*. As many as thirty thousand people in one season visited these popular tourist spots. According to travel and descriptive writers, these hordes were attracted by the broad expanses of lawns in the parklike cemeteries and by the sculptures which were called the cemeteries' architectural triumphs.

An afternoon visit to a scenic cemetery included meditation, walks, and conversation. Popular monuments and the stories behind them aroused travel writers' interests. Legendary and historical figures were particularly acknowledged. As a result of a trip to the cemetery, the antebellum traveler got outdoor exercise before there were a great many parks, enjoyed a ride into the countryside, and was given an opportunity to contemplate death.* It was the natural setting that was most important to the travel writer. Cemeteries were called the loveliest spots on earth, combining picturesque and wild effects which delighted the romantic antebellum mind. Interestingly enough, a cheering influence was said to result from the flowers, shrubs, and shaded lawns. Maria Child thought New York's Greenwood cemetery exceeded Mount

---

*This writer is presently writing a book dealing with nineteenth-century American attitudes toward death, which will analyze more fully the popularity of rural cemeteries, as well as the treatment of death in mass and high culture.

Auburn in natural beauty, and her description of Greenwood contains an aesthetic which was part of the appeal of the rural cemetery for antebellum travelers. She emphasized standing on a high point and seeing a broad vista of New York, the shores of rivers, the sprinkling of villages, the sails of ships, and the margin of the Atlantic.

City inconveniences and evils were duly noted by travel writers, including overcharges for coach hire, overcrowding, noise, dirtiness, poor air, brackish water, crass materialism, and general decadence. For example, William Bobo, a southerner, spoke of the Abbey seven miles from New York where all sorts of fast people and vice could be found. The latter sort of remark is not conspicuous among travel and descriptive writers. Whether it was the tourist, business traveler, emigrant, guidebook writer, or general commentator speaking, his concerns tended to follow major cultural patterns rather than social ones. Therefore, even books written expressly for the pleasure traveler are more than a backdrop for the constructs analyzed in this book. In the essential patterns of pleasure travel, we have already begun to uncover the stance American travel writing took in defining the national character.

3

ARRANGING THE SCENERY

Whether the American traveled for pleasure or business or as a pilgrim, one of the culturally significant characteristics of antebellum travel writing was the sacred ceremony of describing American natural scenery. Tocqueville maintained that democratic societies turned to describing streams and mountains as gods and heroes became inappropriate in an egalitarian setting. Encouraged by the work of landscape painters and by the writings of Cooper, Irving, and minor figures, a romantic and nationalistic interest in nature description developed in popular writing of the era. Travel and descriptive writers felt this interest had not been widely enough cultivated or deeply felt, and really was confined to a small group of literati. Travel writers, thus, decided to educate the masses in the matter of appreciating scenery. Too many tourists, it was believed, went to the White Mountains unable to tell a maple from a beech, an aspen from a birch, or a fir from a pine tree. Scenery hunters had to be taught what to look for and how to react to scenic beauty once it was found. Always ready to be led in these matters, the national mind turned to describers and travelers for guidance.

Travel writers believed a heavy emphasis on practical concerns in antebellum culture was too often ruling out deep responses to nature among Americans. Some writers found nature lavishing her beauties uselessly. No one sang about nature's primitive glories in America. Too often the masses showed no innate sense of beauty and admired or became enraptured exactly where fashion and guidebooks instructed them to. The travel and descriptive writers found their fellow Americans in their daily pursuits looking at nature from a utilitarian and unromantic standpoint. What was a picturesque, unsettled setting to many Americans but something terrible and ugly—crags, lakes, and mountains? For too many Americans natural phenomena were not worth the bother of even a short pilgrimage, according to travel writers. After all, had not Colonel William C. Croghan gone to Europe to learn about Mammoth Cave, although he lived only ninety miles from it? (Croghan bought the cave for ten thousand dollars when he returned.) Travel and descriptive writers knew they had a formidable task before them as they attempted to introduce the national consciousness to the delights of scenery appreciation.

When Americans did go scenery hunting, travel writers found them unaffected by nature's restorative powers. Catskill Falls were turned on and off at a fee for pleasure parties. The American tourist was declared to be a fatuous scenery hunter. He loved nature theoretically, but it was hoped among the travel writers that with education the masses could not remain insensible to the grandeur of nature. It was difficult for some writers to understand that for the American mind survival came first. Therefore, it is not surprising to find reports in travel and descriptive books of Americans who rejected poetic descriptions of natural scenery. Starr King found a New Hampshire man who dismissed a splendid play of light on the mountains. He said to King, "It's nice, but we often have 'em . . ." and returned to hauling stones with his oxen. Another man told King when asked if he were not inspired to dwell in view of the towering mountains about

him, "Blast 'em . . . I don't look at 'em for weeks at a time."
King suggested the great summits must look grand in winter,
but the man retorted, "Guess not, it's too 'tarnal cold. You
come and see the same clouds whirling round them peaks
three weeks at a time, and you'd wish the hills was moved
off and dumped somewhere else."

Travel writers found antebellum scenery hunters bolted
their nature somewhat as they bolted their food. Americans
did the sights with a great rush, gobbled up views, and annihilated landscape. They went to Niagara and ran hurriedly
about for a few hours and went away. Travel writers held
that the real lover of nature rambled leisurely and let nature
unveil the charms of its wildness. Scenery enjoyment had to
be taken seriously, almost from a sacramental posture. It
was as foolish to speed along in a stage through scenery as
it would be to have one's dinner concentrated in a pill, writers
averred.

The national consciousness revealed another side of itself
in travel writings by demonstrating a keen interest in the
bizarre or the freakish in nature, the so-called natural curiosity. Actually, the term "natural curiosity" was an antebellum
catchword broadly applied to famous natural landmarks such
as Mammoth Cave or an exotic plant in Mr. Barnett's
museum and garden of curiosities at Niagara. The American
overemphasized aberrations in nature and lost sight of the
noble and spiritual grandeur which a natural phenomenon like
the profile in the White Mountains held. It was reported that
tourists collected and bought specimens for their own cabinets
of curiosities at home. Hotel and resort spots usually had little
museums of curiosities for the amusement of guests. The taste
for the bizarre showed itself in harsher ways also. Wellington
Williams reported a baby bear was thrown over Niagara Falls
for the enjoyment of tourists; *Pecks' Tourist's Companion* told
of a schooner with animals aboard being sent over the falls for
the novelty of the spectacle and to satisfy the curiosity of
fifteen thousand tourists. On another occasion the vessel
Superior shot over the falls, but no life was sacrificed for the

amusement of tourists, *Pecks'* reported. The significance of these incidents and these attitudes toward nature for the national character can not be minimized when we look at the latter events and consider whether they were sacrifices or examples of brutality. One must be wary in judging the humane standards of one era by those of another. Nevertheless, the meaning of mass attitudes toward nature need to be juxtaposed to the philosophical transcendental attitudes toward nature discussed later in this essay; but at this point we will continue to fill out the picture of mass attitudes toward nature as given to us by travel and descriptive writers.

The manner of describing nature used by travel and descriptive writers is a key to the quality of American attitudes toward nature. Travel writers, although attempting to educate the public, had also to please them and somewhat respond to or develop channels of sympathy about nature. A significant number of writers used a relatively limited group of describers of American scenery; this group included Henry R. Schoolcraft, James Hall, Thomas Jefferson (his description of Natural Bridge was used frequently), James Fenimore Cooper (descriptions by Natty Bumppo were cited often), Nathaniel Parker Willis, and popular professional travel book writers. Some travel writers consciously sought to use American writers. In *The Pioneers,* when Cooper had Natty describe an idyllic scene, a criticism of the machine was combined with an exaltation at confronting nature's vitality. The key line in the passage is, "But the hand that made that 'Leap' never made a mill!" But Cooper's description also captured the movement and life of water. There is no personification or pathetic fallacy actually, but the description has a sacramental character. Antebellum Americans were led to believe that they should find their points of observation and from seeing nature learn something about their inner selves. Nature was the medium through which the natural character was to be filtered and defined. Cooper's description is representative of the passages travel and descriptive books chose to illustrate the American genius for description, but beyond their praising nature description the writers unconsciously were codifying a pathway to the national identity.

It would be misleading to leave the reader with the belief that the Cooper sacramental approach to nature crowded out other methods of describing nature which also had cultural meaning. Antebellum nature description in travel writing also embraced sentimental responses to nature, and these sentimental delineations were constructed of such stock phrases as "overwhelming fury, tumultuous foam, majestic or towering summit, ethereal expanse, luminous gloom, cathedral solemnity, gurgling freshness, austere grandeur, sublime, and properly picturesque." Ecstatic responses are plentiful among travel writers. Effete and genteel pencilings used terms like "grandeur," "picturesque," and "sublime" without much discrimination, and often slipped into pious references to God. Consider in *Our Summer Retreats* the dilation over the picturesque appearance of Weir's Cave in Virginia:

Profound darkness broods over these silent halls... the vastness of the dark vault overhead is only rendered apparent by torches, which render visible, but cannot pierce or dispel the deep obscurity. All who visit the cavern speak of it as being grand and sublime beyond description.

The latter statement contains symbols for the unconscious mind of the mass reader. The cave is grand and sublime, meaning fearsome, because nature's brooding obscurity cannot be easily pierced.

Often nature description which was popularized by travel writers tended to be delicate and stylized, but at its most effective level, culturally speaking, nature description evoked a sense of destiny and touched the spaciousness, unity, and awesomeness of nature which was the national vision of it and the national consciousness of its self. At Elk Lake, the fountainhead of the Mississippi, Charles Lanman created for his readers a wilderness landscape containing the popular pictorial elements and cultural symbols. Lanman's panorama contains the spiritual atmosphere and vessel for national identification—a quiet, solitary place in the woods. Nature is unseen but in harmony around him. An eagle is perched on an old tree, a symbol of time. The eagle ascends, and Lanman shares with the eagle a truly prophetic vision of the culture's unity and grandeur. Nature offers a prayer in the midst of this sacramental experience. The whole of the American search for self-consciousness and self-awareness is contained in Lanman's wilderness portrait and is repeated by other travel and descriptive writers.

Some writers voiced an interest in seeing nature described more robustly. Writers contributed restrained romantic responses as well as sentimental ones. An example of a restrained and graphic description is contained in the following, written by James Hall and quoted by Grenville Mellen:

A roaring and crackling sound [of the prairie fire] is heard like the rushing of a hurricane. The flame, which in general rises to the height of about twenty feet, is seen sinking and darting upwards in spires, precisely as the waves dash against each other, and as the spray flies up into the air; and the whole appearance is often that of a boiling and flaming sea, violently agitated. The progress of the fire is so slow, and the heat so great, that every combustible object in its course is consumed.

The writers allowed sentimental and stylized descriptions and realistic delineations to stand side by side. Both the shallow and the personal, immediate, and genuine response to nature were accepted. The mass culture needed to mature considerably beyond a survival-subsistence basis before being fully able to support a nature aesthetic; and the dissonance in the antebellum approach to nature suggests a psychological uncertainty regarding the appropriateness of a national aesthetic when the *real* experience with nature seemed so harsh.

Travel and descriptive writers unknowingly served as intermediaries between mass culture's hesitancy to accept a full nature aesthetic as part of the national character and the full acceptance of it by the major transcendentalists. One is confronted in reading travel writings with expressions of a deep reverence for the primitive wilderness. These expressions were part of the antebellum allegiance to a philosophy of nature. Often through this philosophy Americans tried to identify their experience and destiny with primitive nature. In popular travel writing the mass mind manipulated this philosophy to suit transitory and conflicting goals. Because of developments in science and technology, the culture slowly sensed a measure of control over the forces of nature and confronted the howling wilderness with a growing courage and with a nature aesthetic, highly refined in the writings of major romantics and tending to the maudlin among the popular writers. More contradictions arose in the mass culture because it was finding its manner of expression, whereas the high culture was secure stylistically.

Travel writers made reverential references to plains not yet trod by the white man and to the experience of wandering through woods where trunks of the primeval forest were still standing. The typical writer asserted that art or the subduing hand of man was unable to add anything to the delight experienced in the wilderness. Thomas Addison Richards in making the following plea absurdly merged the sentimental and primitive response:

Give me the music of the rifle in the untrodden wilderness, and let me gossip with the red-man, the bison, and the bear. What is the crackle of anthracite to the blaze of the burning prairie, or the strains of a guitar compared with the jocund serenade of hungry wolves! Here, far away from the conventionalities and the artificial needs and cares of life, is the place for genuine enjoyment. Here, where your trusty gun may bring you dainty meats for food and warm skins for clothing, beyond which you feel no other wants!

Richards' words were published in a sentimentally decorated gift book, a so-called summer book, and his statement is the stuff of popular mythology. Travel and descriptive writers spread the belief that nature in her primitive state was worth more than all of man's art. From this perspective, art, the civilized, did not rival natural beauty, the primitive.

The worship of natural wildness among travel writers is exemplified by a primitivistic concern for place names in their books. After all, "Chocorua" was a rich and sonorous word, its rhythm evoking the wilderness and the loneliness of the

White Mountains and the sound of the winds moving through
mountain pines. One had for a moment to put aside the hard-
ship of extracting a living from the New Hampshire land. In
bemoaning the lack of imagination in American place naming
and suggesting keeping original and richer Indian names,
travel writers expressed a primitivistic ideology for the masses
and assuaged the consciousness the culture had of its born-
yesterday quality.

Travel writers were concerned over the loss of wilderness
before an advancing civilization. The taming of the wild
horses of Assateague Island was lamented. Everything poetical
in American life seemed to be draining out of it, and this sense
of loss came before the Civil War! The writers expressed regret
at the loss of wild horses, the spoiling of natural beauty, and
the loss of isolated preserves of nature. They feared the wilderness would be crisscrossed by highways and crammed with
homes and boarding houses. It was accepted that in the East
the wilderness had been lost forever, and steamboats and
railroads were poor compensation for the former majesty of
the Hudson. Travel writers saw the advantages of internal
improvements, but they could not accept the destruction of
the culture's symbolic ego ideal, primitive nature.

Nature as a symbol in travel and descriptive writing
performed complex cultural tasks. It was a benevolent and
teaching force. The writers believed that men degenerated
from infrequent contacts with physical nature. Nature was
God's open book to be studied by men. It had more to say
than the marketplace or the great city. Dandies were made
manlier and healthier by going into the wilderness. Men were
made normally better by close contact with nature. Reverence
for nature frequently assumed an aspect of intense religiosity.
Responses to nature were framed by spiritual trappings, and
the era developed a popular idiom in which lofty trees became
stately temple columns, the colors of leaves reminded travel
writers of Gothic cathedrals, and the wind in the forest had
the effect of a great church organ. The sound of Niagara called

forth a mystical religious experience, and after listening to the falls one might chant, "Niagara, Niagara, Niagara!"

The popular mind could not help but be affected deeply and solemnly by nature, according to travel and descriptive writers, and nature would lead one to contemplate and understand God and the whole universe. Nature would reassure man that the world was orderly and comprehensible. Man had only to study nature to know God's wisdom. Frequently, a fearsome side of nature encouraged expressions of reverential piety and awe among travel writers. God's power revealed in nature demanded the same trembling the Puritan felt in confronting the howling wilderness. As a result, travel and descriptive writers gave their readers exclamations of solemn adorations, holy raptures, and emotional responses to the terrible characteristics of nature. Nature charmed the eye with dread, the mind with astonishment, and the soul with awe. The man was not to be envied who could look upon Niagara unmoved; nor was he to be admired who saw no dread in the sublime display of the falls. The cataract became for travel and descriptive writers an emblem of divine power which commanded reverence. Attempting to describe the feelings which Niagara aroused seemed an insurmountable task to the travel writer. He could only compare nature's power to all of life's mysteries—the soul, creation, death.

In their books, travel and descriptive writers guided readers from a feeling of awe before an all-powerful God to a feeling of humility or nothingness in the presence of that powerful God. The moon and stars proved man was nothing and impotent. His material competence—hogsheads of whale oil, tons of spermaceti, pipes of gas—paled before God's cosmic creation. Trenton Falls at flood time proved man was feeble in relation to God's power revealed in the tremendous rush of waterpower. Nature led man to understand, "I am nothing." The poems quoted by travel writers return to the latter theme time and time again.

Coinciding with attitudes of reverence and awe toward nature, another attitude in the national mind was expressed in travel writing. Nature was also considered an enemy. The forest had been a formidable obstacle from the beginning of the American experience. The colonists had cut their way through nature with fierce determination. It was too much to expect the antebellum American who still fought the howling wilderness to accept easily and respond fully to a philosophy of nature or a nature aesthetic which denied his immediate experience or denied his cultural memory. Antebellum westering involved a brutal battle with nature; survival in the West meant subduing nature. Reflecting an unconscious understanding of this attitude, travel writers chronicled the traditions of colonial pioneer horrors resulting from a harsh wilderness. Contemporary western and eastern natural disasters claimed a special interest in travel literature. Just as the Lisbon earthquake confronted philosophical optimism, the antebellum nature aesthetic confronted the facts of the Willey tragedy, the Donner Party, and dozens of accounts of frontier horrors.

The Willey tragedy in the White Mountains was widely discussed during the era. The Willey family was destroyed in 1829 by one of a number of avalanches which occurred in the early nineteenth century. Ironically, the Willeys would have been unharmed had they not abandoned their home. The number of tourists to the White Mountains increased after these avalanches. Travel writers discussed such occurrences; for example, it was reported a student became deranged after he climbed Natural Bridge. Travel writers were not wont to leave unmentioned a curious natural calamity or even a simple drowning. At work in these commentaries are attempts to reconcile conflicting ideas about nature and reality and an attempt to put the reconciliation into the framework of the American self-consciousness. At Genesee Falls writers spoke of the spot where Sam Patch failed to triumph over nature and met his death. George William Curtis described how a young man and child were swept over Niagara Falls. The young man picked up his child and swung her over the water not far from the falls. They were laughing gaily and the child feigned fright when suddenly she fell into the rapids. The father jumped in and caught his daughter in his arms, but the slippery stones on the water bottom joined with the current's force made the father lose his foothold, and he and his child were swept over the falls.

This extensive interest in natural calamities and tragedies formed part of an intricate complex of cultural attitudes toward nature which the antebellum mind manipulated and tried to order. To understand the intricacy of this complex, one has only to juxtapose the memory of the colonial tradition of a howling wilderness and the immediate reality of the antebellum experience with a harsh and horrible nature to the culture's attempt to explain itself through a philosophy of nature—often a broadly defined primitive nature, sometimes a pastoral nature.

The belief that nature was fundamentally unfriendly to man is revealed in the fearsome terms used to describe it. In a poem by a Reverend C.H.A. Bulkley entitled "Niagara," quoted in Sherman's *Trenton Falls,* nature is set forth with such expressions as "hoarse strains," "desolate wail," "anguish," and "fiercely." (In the Abby A. Rockefeller Folk Art Gallery in Williamsburg, Virginia, there is an Edward Hicks painting on a fireplace board which includes a view of Niagara Falls and a few lines from Alexander Wilson's *The Foresters.* In the lines chosen fearsome terms like "dread" stand out.) Writers described fearful precipices, and prepared tourists to respond to the awfulness and chaos of savage scenery. Nature could be an old tyrant and the wilderness not very pleasant. George Wilkins Kendall feared nature when he said that on the prairie man was *in* the world, but not part of it, for in the midst of its isolation he saw no indication of other human beings inhabiting the earth on which he stood. Kendall found none of the romantic fancy of nature poetry for companionship or comfort on the lonely, endless prairie. There was a distinction between the poet's nature and the real nature, and some writers wanted the difference acknowledged. Randolph Marcy claimed that the culture's military institution served to unite "the chasm between the culture of civilization in the aspect of science, art, and social refinement, and *the powerful simplicity of nature."* The simplicity Marcy referred to had a harsh, thumping character for the national consciousness. In filling in the outlines of the national reality, this simplicity added dark, foreboding strokes which Melville in *Moby Dick* chose to study, making it indeed, as he called it, a black book.

A fear of nature helped complicate the American double allegiance to a philosophy of primitive nature on one hand and to the subjugation of nature on the other. Travel writers emphasized considerably the American experience of subduing the wilderness. James Hall, John Hayward, and other writers wrote reassuringly of the certain victory and significant rewards which would come to those who proclaimed war against the forest. Describing his travels in Maine, James Russell Lowell enjoined Americans to accept their current destiny in the workshop until the American struggle with nature was over and the shaggy continent was tamed. Further, travel writers believed that the national mind was being educated in the course of subduing the wilderness. The need to subdue nature was turned into a formative process in the development of the national character. Progress for the writers included triumph over nature.

The nature aesthetic propounded in summer and gift books had to take second place in travel writing to an approach which valued the use of nature to secure comfort and wealth. What Americans valued was the fact that Pittsburgh was rich in mineral resources. They wanted travel books to tell them that. The weight of ideas in travel writing leads one to conclude that survival was the first order of business in the national mind. The survival approach to nature was a pattern long-established in the national character, and the most crucial element when it came to evaluating and acting upon reality. The other seemingly contradictory allegiance to primitivism was necessary to the total view of the national self. The American character could only be realized, defined, and understood through a perpetual battle with nature. Primitive nature had to be preserved only to be subdued. Inevitably, the national mind found it difficult to deal with its ultimate destruction in the present or future.

American travel writers understood that miners did not waste time climbing peaks to dilate over nature. Charles Lanman, upon questioning a frontiersman on the sportsman-like way of killing deer, was told that animals were meant to supply man with food and how they were killed did not matter. The American was described as pitting his needs and energies against those of nature. The life of a forest or of a mountainside was inferior to man's vital energies. Resources of nature were intended to be used to advance the American on a rapid and grand march to power. Henry Ward Beecher accepted antebellum America as a utilitarian age and declared the first and foremost use of nature was the industrial-commercial use. Grass was for hay, flowers were for medicine, springs were for dairies, rocks were for quarries, and trees were timber. Thereafter Beecher and other writers could accept the use of nature for science and literature. Objects in nature were connected to commercial and domestic economies, and beyond that, the national character found for them meanings which were less central. Modern, mass American man imposed his harmonies on the world; he did not look within the world to find his place in a predetermined harmony.

The latter idea was bothersome to travel writers, and because of this bother the same books which praised man's subjugation of nature also complained of man's misuse of nature. In some ways the substance of this criticism was less straightforward than the beeline, utilitarian thinking travel writers found among their fellow Americans. Therefore, travel and descriptive writers often shifted from playing a role as reinforcers of the national consciousness to the role of reformers of the national mind. Writers as a group complained that Mammon came first in American culture. Mrs. Child bemoaned the loss to speculators of Brooklyn Heights where instead of a promenade, stores and a wharf were being built.

The writers lamented the destruction of American primeval beauty by commercialism and the sweeping tide of population.

The writers realized that somehow primitive nature had to be preserved to insure the establishment and survival of a national character. They warned their readers to take precautions; they became Cassandras. The marring of nature by men at Genesee Falls, at Baltimore, in Michigan, and elsewhere was condemned. The writers complained of railroads slashing the American scenery and rejected this action as improvement. In Maine, Theodore Winthrop, watching acres of great pine logs floating in the Penobscot River, realized what Maine men thought timber was made for, and he concluded after visiting Old Town that the lordly pines had been growing for centuries only to be cut up by shrieking gang-saws and gnashed into boards and chewed into sawdust. There is no mistaking his lament, but his complaint was at least a century too late, because certain patterns fixed in the national character in our early history were reinforced with a vengeance during the antebellum period. These attitudes were codified as the national character was defined. There was no turning back.

Nevertheless, the responses of travel and descriptive writers form an interesting body of thought attempting to work the national character in and out of a maze of conflicting attractions and postures. Horace Greeley described a fire in which men died because a few reckless men set the woods afire out of curiosity. Greeley took the opportunity to complain in his book about the disappearance of timber resources, and he predicted the eventual extinction of the redwoods. Travelers who went south deplored the old belief that the land would not wear out. Writers commented about the denuded American patrimony, the loss of forests, buffalo, deer, moose, etc. Primitive nature had to be protected as well as preserved. It was natural to use a tree for fuel or timber, but selective use insured the growth of young trees, and a man who cut down large, healthy trees adjoining a road or in a field was considered an unpardonable vandal. Henry Ward

Beecher believed the well-grown tree a noble thing, the only art treasure of an American community. Margaret Fuller scorned a man who walked up to Niagara Falls, looked at the falls as though he were considering a way to appropriate them for his own use, and then spat into the waters. Clearly, a balance or resolution of elements in the national character was needed.

In the cultural syndrome of identifying the national self with primitive nature, the travel writer had to balance one force against the other—reverence for nature, fear of nature, warnings of the misuse of nature, and assurance of preservation—to keep the mass cultural psyche functioning. The fact that the American land was extremely fertile and the widespread belief that resources were inexhaustible were used in travel writing to blunt the significance of the aggressive and destructive antebellum approach to nature. The writers made millennial predictions about natural resources. The gold mines surely would not be exhausted in a thousand years, and Horace Greeley remarked that the amount of mining done by 1859 was "very much what tickling an elephant's ear with a pin would be toward dissecting him." One pioneer told Charles Fenno Hoffman with typical western exuberance and exaggeration that his farm had pretty good gravelly loam of eighteen inches; but he was considering moving on to Kalamazoo where he heard the soil was four feet deep and greasy fat. Travel writing contains references to countless buffalo, deer, etc., revealing a culture posture which assumed endless plenty.

The writers helped spread myths about the fertility of the American soil. Readers were told about the most prolific soil in the world which only required the passing of a plough over the top to be prepared for planting. Over and over it was repeated that American natural resources were endless; for example, it was declared that the Cumberland coal region could supply the entire world for more than forty thousand years; writers felt one could cut and haul wood and logs until eternity without the supply being exhausted. Optimistic accounts in travel literature of coal beds, peat, marl, granite, etc., echoed a traditional optimism about the inexhaustible American plenty, which went back to colonial travel writers of the seventeenth and eighteenth centuries.

Illusions about endless plenty joined with substantial advancements in technology and industrialism to play a major part in the development of the national character. The culture's philosophy of nature met head-on with the machine. Travel writers recorded the destruction of natural beauty which accompanied the machine, and they considered in their books whether or not nature was being made to subserve the paltriest uses. What was to be the relationship between the beautiful waterfall and sledgehammers, nail cutters, mill stones, and cotton jennies? Cataracts turned without losing a drop of profit for speculators. It is not surprising, then, to find Robert Montgomery Bird in *The Hawks of Hawk Hollow* (1835) crying out that the Greeks would have created a God to live under Niagara while the American satisfied himself with clapping a paper mill just above it. The smoky purlieus of Wheeling, Charles Fenno Hoffman observed, were unattractive to all except the man of business. Pittsburgh had the dirty smoke that came with a mill town and to Americans that smoke was a sign of progress, but travel writers complained about the machine as a tyrant.

The conflict between the machine and nature was sometimes dramatized by describing the harsh sound of machinery. Visitors to factories found the clanking iron noises disconcerting. William T. Thompson, "Major Jones," in his travel sketches, found the machinery of a New England whip factory "whirlin and whizzin, rattlin and dashin, as if it would tear everything to pieces." The humorist here is uncovering the dark fears the culture felt at the beginning of the Industrial Revolution when the national character was being defined. The personification of the machine, especially the railroad engine, in fearsome terms by travel writers tells us that for Americans the machine, at least unconsciously, was considered a monster, one to be dealt with and assimilated cautiously into the national consciousness. Committed to a philosophy of primitive nature at least in popular art and tradition, Americans understood how the force of technology was a double-edged sword. It created and might destroy the source and focal point of the national identity. Symbolically, travel and descriptive writers brooded over the force and speed of railroad cars and suspected no earthly power could stop them. The railroad meant heat, bustle, and dust. It meant nervous activity. It was described as a jointed reptile or fearsome beast. For Henry Ward Beecher it was a modern thunder dragon dragging its tail. In describing a train plowing through snow using two fiery dragons or engines, Beecher, as did other travel writers, uncovered the machine's effect on the American psyche. The event contained energetic action, irresistible power, darkness and light, and fitful half-lights. There was excitement in the action of the two engines. They stirred the imagination. They whirled into the storm, sped with wild force through open fields and deep forests, plunged into dark caves, wrestled through dreary recesses, emerged again with screaming whistles. In the end the trains ran past the station, had to be choked down and reined back into the depot. Certainly, Beecher's engine is not the "punctual as a star" machine Emily Dickinson described in her well-known poem. The speed of steam machines frightened some travel writers; others favored punctual and controllable machines or straddled the fence and declared fear of the potential for getting out of control and joy in the machine's useful power. The question was whether happiness lay in being moved mentally and physically with great rapidity. Americans had to know they were to be happy.

Once again, balancing the different parts of its reality and trying to formulate a coherent national self-portrait, writers did not completely reject the machine. Often overlooking their own criticisms and fears, they accepted technology and industrialism. The steam engine was described as accomplishing formidable tasks, developing industries which freed the United States of European economic servitude, and helped tame the harsh wilderness. No doubt wanting to believe the supply of natural resources was inexhaustible helped writers to embrace modern technology as beneficial. In addition, the writers reassured their readers that there were no European-like industrial slaves here; unlike English operatives, the Lowell girls had no intention of working in the factory indefinitely. Melville's *Redburn* stated this position as fact as he surveyed the horrors of Liverpool, so much was the idea made a cultural dictum. The evils of industrialism were minimized by writers; the willingness to accept industrialism evidences itself clearly. Thus, Charles Goodrich stated flatly that manufacturing was America's dominant interest after agriculture. Lorenzo Bowen boasted Boston's decided predilection for manufactures. The dam crossing the Connecticut River at Holyoke, Massachusetts, became in *Our Whole Century* a triumph of art over nature, forecasting Holyoke's future as a great manufacturing city. As I observed in an early chapter, tours of manufacturing establishments were prescribed visiting points for tourists. Mills with their accompanying steam engines were described in order to evoke national pride; they symbolized material and general advancement. Travel and descriptive writers hammered away at this theme. For example, they wrote about forty different manufacturing companies which used steam power in Cincinnati. Pittsburgh was dirty and noisy, but it was proclaimed the Birmingham of America. Every mechanic of any standing, it was to be believed, had a steam engine working for him. These engines were economical, did the work of thousands, and might well be included in the population estimate of any town. They were described as proud and noble servants. American technology was said to afford a theme for the American muse. The steam engine had a poetic mystery about it.

According to travel and descriptive writers, the West looked forward to the promises of industrialism also. So widespread was this feeling about the place of technology and industrialism in the American self-portrait that even the preserve of primitive nature was described to readers of travel and descriptive books as being anxious to encourage manufacturing enterprise. Travel writers explained how western states in their infancy could not be expected to produce much in the line of machinery and manufactures, but the West was on the alert, understood the place of industrialism in the national future, and it was prepared to assimilate an industrial posture in the midst of decidedly antithetical roles it was given to play in unfolding the national drama.

Many of these attitudes account for the mania about railroads which American travel writers found as they went abroad in their own land. The locomotive, the steam engine especially, became enmeshed with the symbols which expressed the vitality and triumph of republican institutions. Travel writing frequently used the railroad to express that vitality and triumph. Anne Royall after an exhilarating railroad ride exclaimed, "I shall ever, after this, be the warm advocate of railroads! Railroads! Railroads! give me a railroad!" She was amused to see birds, cats, dogs, and cows fly for their lives before the oncoming train. The railroad more than any other technological development underlined the go-ahead, activist character of Americans, and when the building of railroads was proposed anywhere the prospect was greeted jubilantly. Railroads were indications of America's progress and enterprising character.

The enthusiasm for railroads encouraged elaborate railroad celebrations, optimistic forecasts about the American destiny, and a general feeling of national exuberance and self-confidence. Travel literature recorded these cultural developments with religious scrupulousness. The reports took on an apocalytic tone; the country was being traversed by grand bands of iron, which were described as truly wonderful. But those bands did much more than create a sense of wonderment. They symbolized for many travel writers an indestructible band of union for the culture. The projected transcontinental railroad was believed to have the potential to forge a stronger union, increase material prosperity, and uplift the moral character of the American mind. Thus, the railroad became a unifying element in travel and descriptive writing; it was to make possible a lesser fear of nature and contribute to the spiritual growth of the country. Behind these ideas was the concern to find in the society's reality a stable, comprehensible national character. One did not need to be able to articulate such a cultural construct with precision; it had to be felt mystically and filtered through the general consciousness emotionally. Why should not Americans assume the risks of industrialism when the machine held promise as well as fears? Perhaps it is inevitable for a culture, as for an individual, to be drawn to action where both elements, fear and promise, exist. Had not Jonathan Edwards moved toward true virtue with a feeling of joy and fear?

The romantic mass posture found poetic the straight lines of the railroad which pierced the landscape. These lines cleaved the country to the single point. In the wilderness one forgot the prosaic quality of the railroad. Not even poets sighed for old stagecoach days. Indirectly, a new poetry of speed was demanded by travel writers, although they might on an earlier page in their books have dilated over the leisurely quiet of sailing. Consider Melville's use of the railroad when Ahab says at the end of the "Sunset" chapter, "Swerve me? The path to my fixed purpose is laid with iron rails, whereupon my soul is grooved to run." And in *Walden*, the chapter entitled "Sounds," we find Thoreau talking about being a "track-repairer in the orbit of the earth" and being shouted off the track as a locomotive approaches. Thoreau claimed Americans had constructed "an Atropos, that never turns aside." Also, we have the interesting difference between the two rivers in Twain's *Life on the Mississippi* (1883), the untamed, primitive antebellum river and the tamed-by-the-Army-Corps-of-Engineers river of the post–Civil War era. Twain regretted the loss of the former, of course.

Finally, in using nature to interpret their culture's character, experience, and destiny in the face of a dynamic industrialism, the mass of travel and descriptive writers presented a complex view of the national character. Putting aside differences among the writers, the common feature of their writing is the attempt to face the same problem and contradictions in similar cultural terms, constructs, and rationalizations, some subtle, others shallow. [In unconscious attempts to reconcile the machine and nature, travel writers saw the improvements of technology as uniting emphatically beauty and utility and thereby encompassing the full human spirit.] Some writers thought the loom might be too strong for the plow, but an attempt to merge all the irreconcilables into a national character with nature as a matrix was typical. From the standpoints of travel and descriptive writers, Americans worshiped at the shrine of Niagara and dilated over sentimental descriptions of American scenery in gift books, maintaining a position of respect for nature as they exploited it. Their humility before the evidence of God's force revealed in nature was set beside a feeling of pride and power expressed in subjugating nature with the help of the machine.

This complex of responses to the environment and new reality reported and discussed in travel writing moved in erratic ways. The complex zigged and zagged to accommodate itself to an Edenic-materialistic idea, that is, in this garden of the world, the land of plenty, everyone was to have his chance to get rich. Although there was uncertainty regarding America's proper correspondence with nature, a final reconciliation between primitive nature and civilization was acknowledged as an important antebellum objective and article of belief. Henry Tanner in his popular book *View of the Valley of the Mississippi* (1834) echoed an idea expressed in many books of travel and description when he said that because nature appeared everywhere on a grand scale in the United States, it would influence Americans toward noble conceptions and impress its own image of greatness on the American character. Tanner realized that wild nature alone was impotent as an influence if it were not joined to culture. So joined, Tanner and other writers believed, nature would create true greatness in the American. There was not to be chaos, incomprehensibility about reality, irrationality in facing reality, on the pathway to fixing the exact points of the national character.

The American could be confident, because his self and his reality were coherent and manageable. Modern complex cultures must have a sense of stability and permanence, American culture more than others.

4

~~~~~~

INSECURITY AND STABILITY

~~~~~~

Reconciling the conflicting positions Americans held about nature did not bring complete security and stability to the national mind. Cultural confidence is not quickly acquired, and no braggadocio could relieve the American's uneasiness regarding his cultural identity. A great deal of cultural machinery was needed to rid Americans of a deep sense of inferiority vis-à-vis European wealth, history, tradition, and literature. One way of dealing with the problem was to camouflage a sense of cultural insecurity. Travel and descriptive writers used various postures to counter the insecurity. These postures include trumpeting the rapid growth and the newness of the country, that is, turning a disadvantage to an advantage by saying it was so; predicting millennial future progress for the culture; and promoting America. By underlining growth, predicting future progress, and promoting America, travel writers gained for the culture a measure of self-assurance as its European parent watched, and more importantly, insured the culture a predictable reality.

In discussing growth writers left no doubt that material development in America was *rapid*. Lawrence, Massachusetts, was described as a city built in one year, and feverish building continued there. This kind of cultural construct and pattern is what Henry Adams had in mind when he wrote in his monumental *History of the United States* that one of the important elements of the national character is to prefer rapid change to slow evolution. Writers called Lowell, Massachusetts, the Manchester of America and boasted that in 1815 it had been only a wilderness. In Boston, changes and improvements happened so rapidly that old buildings described in a guidebook on sale might have already disappeared, and the pace of enterprise in the city was so feverish that its exterior seemed to writers like the colors of a chameleon, varying constantly. In their books travel writers spread this kind of belief. They told of the rapid change and growth of American cities, and this change and growth was heralded by writers in terms of factories, population increase, and the appearance of general affluence.

Travel writers made the rapid growth of the West appear more dramatic than that in the East. They wrote of the "Great West," and they declared it unequaled in its material growth and making giant strides in moral improvement. Emigrant guides assured readers of the reality of progress in the West; the rapidity with which improvements were completed and the Herculean efforts being made astonished travel writers. Enchantment seemed to be at work; it appeared the United States would soon be filled with millions of free men from the Atlantic to the Pacific, "living under the laws of Alfred, and speaking the language of Shakespeare and Milton," as Samuel Augustus Mitchell, using Coleridge's words, put it.

Travel writers readily told stories about the amazing rapid growth which a western town gained once it was born and baptized. The typical account pointed to a wild and primitive wilderness of a short time before and contrasted it to the number of institutions and people which filled the wilderness at the most recent census. The high spirits of writers exaggerated western growth. On the whole, developments became, for travel books, marvelous and magical. Growth was so rapid and on such a firm and enlightened base that churches and schools sprang up before there were people to fill them, and an historical society was established before an area had a history to record. A town was considered in a pretty mature state if it were six months old, and one might expect plans being made for the construction of a railroad eighteen months after the first white man erected his cabin in a territory. These reports contain the mythic stuff for the development of the national character.

A few writers wondered whether rapid growth could be sustained. Could anyone be so visionary as to believe that the rapid rate of growth would continue for a long time and would not sooner or later decrease? However, such expressions of doubt were not commonplace in the travel literature. Even skeptical writers went on to estimate substantial increases in population and wealth. Everything was too near its infancy to estimate real decline in the long line of progress within the range of the nineteenth century. Whatever slowdown might come or whatever the society's lot might be, nineteenth-century America had a promising future before it, and at least no European decadence was to be found here.

The concept of growth in the United States was very early connected to a fascination with quantity in the national mind. George Santayana in *Character and Opinion in the United States* (1934) wrote that a visitor to Niagara Falls could expect to hear about the number of tons of water falling per second, the number of towns which received power from the falls, and the dollar value of the industries the falls might support. Antebellum travel and descriptive writers understood the meaning of numbers for Americans. Numbers assured Americans of the marvelous state of their culture. Antebellum Americans used numbers—the cost of buildings, statistics on manufacturing and technological innovations, the proliferation of humane and cultural innovations—to advertise and reaffirm the advance of American prosperity and culture. Readers learned, for instance, that the lot on which a bank was built cost fifty thousand dollars, and that this cemetery or that customs house was enclosed by an imposing and costly railing. The cost of canals, capitol buildings, steamboats, hotels, college buildings, as well as any other indication of wealth and prosperity, was emphasized by writers. There was a persistent under-lining of the material value of things.

An emphasis on size by writers was also part of the cultural use of numbers. Statistical charts in the books show the growth of individual cities, the length of railroads in the United States, the value of fisheries; there are statistics on the number of saw mills, the salaries of government officers, the length of pipe in waterworks, and the growth of population. Writers scrutinized with wonder American statistics which changed so rapidly that every two years the figures were no longer valid. San Francisco in 1849 truly exemplified a remarkable example of the sacramental character of numbers. Bayard Taylor told the fable of a man in San Francisco who died $41,000 in debt one autumn; a year later, because the administrators of his estate delayed settling his affairs, the value of his real estate had increase so rapidly that his debts were paid and his heirs had a yearly income of $40,000!

Emphasis on rapid development also involved trumpeting the acquisition of humane and civic institutions. Visiting a benevolent institution shed a bright luster on the culture's citizens, according to travel writers. Mount Auburn was continually pointed to with pride as an example of the advancement of the age and society, and it was usually compared to the Cimetière du Père-Lachaise. Lyceums, charitable associations, religious societies, free reading rooms, atheneums, etc., were listed for individual cities and towns. American institutions compared favorably with any others in the world, and these institutions proclaimed the humane character and the success of the American republic, but they also were assurances which dispelled the culture's sense of insecurity.

Many pronouncements by the writers were optimistic statements of what was to be, rather than what was. The interest in material expansion involved making hopeful prophecies; there was a feeling of expectancy in the books, everything was on the brink of becoming. America's future as well as her present had to be boosted and had to be sold to herself. Belief in American prospects became an act of faith necessary from the members of the culture. It took Americans only three log houses to make a city, but they began calling it a city as soon as they staked out lots. Every small hamlet was certain to make a noise in the world at some time. Using European accomplishment as a criterion, Americans reported their material achievements as outstripping the past and projected them into the future. For example, Americans were told the Croton aqueduct in terms of magnitude of design and solidity outshone all similar modern structures and even rivaled the ancient Roman aqueducts. Furthermore, this American architectural triumph symbolized the liberality and enterprise of a free people and demonstrated that Americans acted for the benefit of future generations. For travel writers Lowell, Massachusetts, represented a harmonious system of industrial power which could be extended indefinitely and for which all Europe afforded no parallel. Thus, American material achievement was boosted as being on a vaster scale than its European counterparts. Grenville Mellen with typical braggadocio declared that excepting Great Britain and Holland no country in the world contained as many or as long canals as did the United States, and that the whole of Europe had not built so much during a period of sixteen years as had Pennsylvania, New York, and Ohio alone. Travel writers found fledgling states joining in vast enterprises such as canals and proclaimed their actions truly national in character.

The psychological effects of antebellum America's inferior position in terms of European wealth and culture were evident throughout travel literature. Consider the effects on the national psyche created by the burning of the American capital in 1814. Americans strained to show themselves a people who existed independently and had a bright future. Nevertheless, the rapid development and continual flux in American culture, which was so well advertised, gave the aspect of glaring newness to antebellum America, and Americans had ambivalent feelings toward this newness. For some, newness was a virtue, and American freshness joined to the grandeur of the American landscape and the vigorous moral character of the people gave us our collective strength. Our newness and the qualities associated with it pointed to an expansive humanity and a higher culture than the world had yet achieved.

Though she believed that out of raw newness would come a new order and a new poetry, Margaret Fuller in her western journey was prepared for the distasteful effects of mushroom growth. She knew that where everything was "go ahead," villages could not grow proportionally, gently, and slowly. The slow nurturing of traditions was impossible here. However, counterbalancing her view, other writers declared that even American impulses were new. Although writers spoke with pride about American newness, there was also anxiety expressed in the books about America's lack of associations and traditions, and they were uncomfortable about the rawness and unsightliness of American newness. A culture which explained itself in terms of perpetual newness and continual flux was faced with the dilemma of securing an important index of culture—a sense of stability and permanence. Paradoxically, the pattern was cut in the period which placed flux and stability side by side in the national self-consciousness. That is why the American consciousness is essentially romantic and fantastic.

Travel writers concluded that too often the beginnings of a civilization are unsightly. A wood half–cut down seemed like a house torn apart. Stumps and rocks jutting out of the ground were dismal and slovenly in a landscape. Newness brought a tiresome and never-ceasing whirl of business, too. Some writers wrote of being tired of improvements and wanting some place finished and peaceful. As a result, writers delighted in the slower-growing southern cities which did not appear as though they had been built yesterday. Charleston's picturesqueness had the semblance of European antiquity for some travel writers. They wondered if mere scenery without historical association is enjoyable but unsuggestive. Writers yearned to find a sense of time and cultural stability which they believed antiquity created.

Although Americans had been told by European commentators that they needed neither a past nor the tone which a past gave to a culture, in travel writing the worship of rapid change and newness existed alongside a desire to create a sense of stability through historical, natural (physical nature), and literary associations. The yearning for such associations is expressed by travel writers who thought of springs which arose adjacent to one another and ultimately discharged in the Atlantic and in the Gulf of Mexico. Such natural phenomena led them to create images of a national unity. These images were often associated with ancient mythologies; a classical aura, thereby, was to be sensed by their readers. American gigantic pines and awesome Niagaras were to inspire new mythologies; Americans could take comfort in possessing the mythic stuff in which stable and secure civilization thrived.

Much of this mythologizing by travel writers took the form of describing and embellishing romantic traditions connected to specific geographic locations. They tried to preserve Indian place names and discourage place naming which negated the development of romantic traditions. There was no doubt that the American mind needed myth and symbol to realize its identity. Although writers might not have said so in such a clinical way, there is no doubt that the question of the need for symbols in a republic like the United States was given direct attention. This attention revealed an understanding of the culture's subtle needs and an understanding of the dilemma an egalitarian society faces when it leaves moral decisions to the conscience of each individual man, each imperfect. The writers understood that the very practical tendency of the American mind to disdain forms made it all the more important to cherish some outer symbols of an inner national soul. In the Jacksonian egalitarian stirrings of antebellum culture, there was an inner cultural rift which on one side found Americans straining for distinctions and emblems and on the other found them philosophically committed to a rejection of social gradation and forms.

The foreign commentators helped create an ambivalance in the American mind about its lacking a sense of time. They pointed to the loss of chronicles, traditions, legends which the break with England reportedly caused. They called the United States a country without a history or monuments. It is not surprising to find travel writers responding to this criticism. They maintained with Emerson that America was of the new, should shed all the effete and corrupt ways of the Old World, and had no need of associations and historical time. Lack of tradition was said to be the nation's outstanding characteristic. It was unnecessary—more, a sacrilege—to venerate the past. Recall that Hawthorne had Clifford say in *The House of the Seven Gables,* "There is no such unwholesome atmosphere as that of an old home, rendered poisonous by one's defunct forefathers and relatives." Americans were to slash ahead and produce new traditions and create a new history by fullfilling their bright destiny. Somewhere in the dim future, perhaps, historical time would find an acceptable place in the national scheme of things. For the moment, had not the United States liberated itself culturally as well as politically from Europe in 1776? Of course, the myth that the nation was culturally free from its European past overlooked the ingrained cultural legacies and patterns of value which it received from Western civilization, but the myth afforded a comfortable cultural rationalization for the rebellion of the adolescent culture against its parent and the establishment of its own identity. Some travel writers, like Henry T. Tuckerman, realized that the myth "minimized fatally the large contributions which European civilization" had made to American culture.

In spite of the attempt to define itself in terms of newness, American culture expressed concern about its lack of historical and traditional associations. As a healthy individual tries to find balance in his reality, American culture sought order in what it called associations. The term implied a whole range of cultural constructs. Our land was said to be larger and grander than the European land, but it could not be studied in detail because it lacked associations. Only science might be permitted such a study. Nevertheless, travel writers spoke of a spacious and stately land, varied and magnificent in outline, epical rather than lyrical. The land without associations implied the continent behind, the possibility always in the future to be and become. One might miss the gray cloisters and ruined towers of Europe on the Hudson, but the American reader was reminded that American scenery was not polluted by memories of past superstitions, ignorance, and crime which filled European memory. Each wooded height and rocky bluff in America, although not crowned by romantic abbeys or castles, nevertheless told of a noble time and holy deeds, told of the Indian, the virgin land, and the Revolution.

Yet we find Mrs. Child expressing an uncomfortable awareness of living in a culture lacking in rich historical emblems. She wondered how anyone could speak of the antiquities of New York. This was a new and constantly changing country. Tradition had no desolate arches or dim cloisters. Americans changed homes so often, that as Washington Irving suggested, their ghosts did not know where to call upon them. Our newness tended to make us an irreverent culture. Phrenologically, the organ of veneration in Americans was said to be very little developed. Instead of cathedrals we had meeting houses simply lighted; instead of cloisters, we had ready-made coffins in shop windows; instead of poetry and philosophy we had Franklin's "Poor Richard," and instead of kings we had administrations turned in and out of office at every election.

Describers of American scenery understood the unsatisfied hunger for a sense of historical time in the national mind. As they looked upon their scenery, travel writers only wanted monuments of antiquity to give it the fullest meaning. Thoreau in *A Week on the Concord and Merrimack Rivers* (1849) displayed more vision and patience, as well as playfulness, when he observed:

Who knows what shape the fable of Columbus will at length assume, to be confounded with that of Jason and the expedition of the Argonauts? And Franklin—there may be a line for him in the future classical dictionary, recording what the demigod did, and referring him to some new genealogy.

In his *Journal* Thoreau discussed Indian relics in such a way as to suggest that they afforded antiquities through which

Americans could soothe their insecure cultural psyches. In *Walden* he mentioned "the ashes of unchronicled nations who in primitive years lived under these heavens." Regarding Thoreau's reference to Franklin above, it is interesting to note that in *Moby Dick* Melville defended the good blood of Nantucket whalemen by tracing their ancestry to Franklin's grandmother. Travel writers attempted to extract from references to historical and traditional events and to national monuments a sense of continuity, stability, and permanence which the young culture lacked but strongly desired. In his introduction to an anthology of American travels, Professor Warren S. Tryon says that the insertion of history into American travels reveals a consciousness that "a land without ruins is a land without memories—a land without memories is a land without history," a quotation from "A Land Without Ruins" (1879) written by the Maryland poet Joseph Ryan (1838–86). Professor Tryon also notes that these excursions into history are unreliable and can be ignored as history; of course, the question of historical accuracy does not bear directly on the thesis presented here, i.e., the creation of history satisfied specific needs of the national mind.

Travel writers enjoyed including in their books some historical details, consciously referring to historical time to create a past for the American scene. They wrote of places known to history for two centuries and spots rich in historical and legendary associations. They found sacred historical recollections clustering over many spots in the country. They missed no opportunities to point out to readers reminiscences of unequaled historical interest, ancient epitaphs, ancient cemeteries, ancient buildings, and Americans who sprang from ancient stock. Nature spots were cried up for their historical significance as well as scenic beauty. Writers sought to include specific traditional tales of heroism, usually dealing with the Revolutionary war. The practice was so widespread and at times blatant that a few writers complained about overdoing the addition of historical and fanciful association to the American scene.

Another aspect of the search for historical time is found in the unconscious attempts to supply, imaginatively, castles in the American landscape. Writers were reminded of the Roman Coliseum and ruined castles upon seeing Rocky Mountain buttes. A lofty crag called to mind the fact that in Europe a castle might stand upon it. Writers had no scruples against using Indian history and tradition to supply a sense of historical time to the American scene, and evidence of the Indian's long presence on the continent was incorporated into travel accounts constantly, ironically, to satisfy the white man's cultural needs. Roy Harvey Pearce points out that the image of the Indian had no intrinsic meaning in early American fiction; but the Indian was used by travel writers as a pathway to white identity. Indian trails trodden for hundreds of years are reverently noted, as well as the location of early remnants of Indian civilizations, civilizations which Americans had been or were destroying. Important landmarks and monuments were to be venerated by Americans; visitors to Niagara were encouraged to make excursions to the ruins of old Fort Erie, and no traveler could leave Washington without making a pilgrimage to Mount Vernon, the sacred spot to which every American mind was enjoined to turn devotedly.

Related to this eagerness to supply their culture with a sense of history, writers complained about the inadequate preservation by Americans of their historical assets. They complained of the neglect of the birthplace of historical figures, of old forts, etc. There was an interest in preserving historical monuments, but travel writers found the culture's practical and business concerns came first. What little history Americans had was sadly neglected, and writers noted that in a country like the United States which had so few antiquities it was melancholy to have historical remnants and landmarks destroyed and disappear forever.

R. L. Midgley told of the neglect and decay of an old Boston landmark, adding that the thoughtful and thoughtless hurried by it and children accustomed to newness and novelty wondered at its strange antiquity. Historical sites were being

destroyed by tearing down old buildings to be replaced by
newer style buildings suited to the nation's commercial growth.
The age and culture were pronounced irreverent and forgetful
by travel writers. Lorenzo Bowen pled to have the Revolutionary forts around Boston preserved as noble monuments of
liberty. The situation was the same in Philadelphia and elsewhere. Modern improvement swept away old buildings, ruins,
and places which might inspire patriotism, encourage genius or
virtue. Had not all other nations venerated such places?

Physical nature satisfied varied national psychological
needs in the period, and at a time when significant advances
in the knowledge of geological time were made, nature became a symbol of antiquity as well as of the new. Charles
Sanford in *Quest for America* states that Benjamin Latrobe's
"well-known corncob and tobacco capitals in the place of the
traditional acanthus leaves for the columns of the Senate
Rotunda seen too artfully, consciously designed for folk art.
Rather, they serve to weld the two themes of the return to
nature and antiquity into a single statement of the national
ideal." Similar associations between time and nature were made
by Thoreau and Melville, in *Walden, A Week on the Concord and Merrimack,* and *Moby Dick.* Travel writers made
geological time an historical association; that is, it was used
to give the culture a sense of historical time. This use of
geological time gave Americans associations which were hoar-
ier and grander than their sparse historical and traditional
ones. Here they felt there was an opportunity to give Europe
stiff competition. Writers continually linked nature to time,
that is, the age of the American continent was emphasized,
suggesting an unconscious attempt to satisfy a basic cultural
desire for permanence through associations connected to time.
Here again the culture was acting very much like the individual in satisfying its needs. These geological associations
assured the culture of its permanence and of stability by placing the age of the American land against the long European
historical past from which the culture had divorced itself.
Italy might have a solid background of antiquity, but Amer-

ica's wild, vast, and beautiful land inspired its citizens and gave inexhaustible sustenance to the culture. In the chapter entitled "The Ponds" in Thoreau's *Walden*, time was cleverly linked to nature:

Perhaps on that spring morning when Adam and Eve were driven out of Eden Walden Pond was already in existence, and even then breaking up in a gentle rain accompanied with mist and a southerly wind, and covered with myriads of ducks and geese, which had not heard of the fall, when still such pure lakes sufficed them.

Thoreau's remark is strikingly similar to the kind found in more prosaic travel and descriptive books.

It is not surprising to find one travel writer after the other proudly announcing the importance of the American continent's age. Had not European geologists themselves acknowledged that the general strata would be determined here? Guidebook writers wondered what chronicles of past ages were niched in the eternal walls of Niagara, and they marveled at the untold ages needed before the Niagara River could have cut a passage through rock for a distance of seven miles. Compared to Niagara, the ruins at Balbec and Palmyra, the pyramids of Egypt, the temples of Greece and Rome, were the toys of time. The Great Stone Face in New Hampshire was described as a sculpture older than the Sphinx, formed thousands of years before Adam. The travel writer invoked the timelessness of nature even by describing centuries-old buffalo paths as vestiges of time. Mark Twain began *Life on the Mississippi* by working brilliantly the same conception of nature and time.

Geologists were quoted frequently concerning the age and origin of the land. Travel writers wrote of wandering along river banks where the waves had heaved for centuries. The character of the American earth was called antediluvian. American antiquities antedated the biblical flood. Trees existed before Christ. Writers asserted that they had rather walk under an ancient American tree than see the noblest cathedral. John Sherman assured his future tourists that by exploring the area around Trenton Falls they would be thrown back spiritually to antediluvian times. Using similar postures, Americans substituted the age of nature for ancient traditions and monuments.

The literary association was also a source of cultural assurance found in travel literature. A conscious effort was made to search out, include, and propose materials to be treated in the national literature, and this search reflects the struggle to achieve literary nationalism and cultural identity. Travel writers called for American lake poets. They wanted their Saco Rivers immortalized. There was a constant boosting of the American scene as a fertile field for literary effort. American poets and painters were told they had a glorious field before them. Had not William Gilmore Simms filled southern woods and plains with mythological creations not unlike those of the ancients? Travel writers collected and attempted to contribute anecdotes, tall tales, folklore, songs, poems, local color, dialect, and folk heroes to American literature, and they acted, therefore, as a latent source of various potentially usable literary materials.

The concern for and interest in hunting up and supplying literary associations was expressed in different ways by travel writers. They did not discriminate finely the sources of specific literary associations; the melting pot principle worked comfortably in this area. It did not matter if the legendary lore being created in America had German, Swedish, or Norwegian origins intermingled with the lore of the Indian; all traditions would somehow merge and become American. In addition to expropriating Indian land literally and symbolically as an historical association, Americans borrowed Indian legends and traditions in creating romantic associations for their own culture. Thus, Indian legends created classic interest in the scenery around Lake Superior. Michigan's newness was mitigated by the vision of the traditional land where ancient Indian hunters saw fairies and genii floating over the lakes and streams and dancing through the forests. To please these fairies and genii was noted as the Indian religion. Travel books included both Indian and American folklore in the cultural process of creating literary associations in the national mind.

Many writers collected folklore materials firsthand and noted the fact. Frequently, the materials collected contained a multiple use of associations, combining a sense of American history, geologic time, and literary implication. Adding to these multiple associations, writers made correlations between classical traditions and American associations. Some travel and descriptive writers quoted contemporary collectors of Indian legends, such as Henry Rowe Schoolcraft and John Treat Irving, Washington Irving's nephew.

The selection of Indian legends and traditions by travel writers is varied and extensive; through it one can compare different layers or versions of Indian folklore. There is much material concerning origins—Indian legends about the origin of San Francisco Bay, the origin of New Jersey, and a deluge legend similar to that in the Bible. Many standard folklore motifs are found, including the lover's leap, the revenge and trick, the test; there are songs and poetry also. Charles Fenno Hoffman took down an Indian serenade as he heard it from an Indian girl. Because he found his translation bald, Hoffman included his own versification of the serenade, and in the process the Indian tradition was fully transferred into the service of antebellum culture's need for a sense of historical time.

In making a point of using American literary materials in delineating the American scene, travel writers alluded to major writers like Cooper, Irving, and Bryant, and referred to minor writers including Nathaniel Parker Willis, Willis Gaylord Clark, James Hall, and Joseph Rodman Drake. Drake's *The Culprit Fay* was frequently cited, no doubt because of the mythological elements which it inserted into the American scene. Descriptions of the Catskills brought forth references to Rip Van Winkle, and readers learned about the Guy Rivers land created by William Gilmore Simms. As travel writers searched out literary associations, capable and third-rate writers were put side by side. There was a conscious effort by writers to pull out of the American scene authentic literary associations.

In addition to using literary allusions to create a sense of national identity, the books contain much incipient literary material, which no doubt was inserted to boost the belief in the fertility of the American literary soil. Writers recorded dialect and thereby answered the foreign traveler's criticism that American life lacked variety and picturesqueness. Travel writers collected tales and anecdotal materials in the course of their peregrinations. One finds tall tales and other types of American humor in travel literature. A tavern keeper told Horace Greeley, "There a'n't nothing bad about this whisky; the only fault is, it isn't good." Greeley used the deadpan attitude to tell his readers about a saloon where visitors had "a careless way, when drunk, of firing revolvers, sometimes at each other, at other times quite miscellaneously, which struck me as inconvenient. . . ." The tradition in the White Mountains was that when furious northwest winds blew in winter two men were needed to hold one man's hair on. Then there were accounts of those who could drive a rusty nail with a rifle at fifty yards or shoot leaves and snowballs from each other's heads. William Cullen Bryant encountered a hunter who was such a good shot that raccoon offered to come out of the trees without giving trouble.

Prosaic gazetteers were not averse to acting as cultural vehicles for tall tales. John Hayward in his *New England Gazetteer* (1839) told the following tradition about Moses Blake, one of the original settlers of Dalton, New Hampshire. Blake was a hunter, famous for his accuracy. He and a Captain Bucknam while hunting fired at a mark not larger than a dollar on a small bet. From the distance of twenty rods, Bucknam fired first and hit the mark near its center. Blake then fired, but upon going to the tree on which the mark was made, he could find no trace of his ball. Bucknam was elated until Blake told him to cut out his ball from the tree and he would find Blake's ball on top of his. Bucknam performed the operation and discovered the truth of Blake's claim. One immediately recalls Cooper's use of a similar motif in the shooting match scene of *The Pathfinder* (1840).

Frederick Law Olmsted recorded a fine example of western humor in a drover's tale. Two drovers talked about the presence and absence of morality in the Red River area. One told the other about a "high old dream" he had had the night before. He had dreamed he was in Hell. Upon being asked if it were rough country, he told of boggy sulphur places and doors which led him right up to the "old boss Devil" asleep "on a red hot sofy." The devil awakened and asked the drover who he was and where he was from. The drover told him where he was from, and the devil said that he thought so and asked him what was going on around Red River. The drover told the devil there was "a protracted meeting" there. The devil quickly called the drover a liar, but was soon convinced by the drover and began to put on his boots to go and break up the meeting. Suddenly he asked who started the meeting, and he was told Elder Slocum, whereupon he stopped putting on his boots and said there was no use in his going if Elder Slocum was around.

Accounts of legends dealing with heroism in the French and Indian and Revolutionary wars were popular with travel writers. For instance, several different versions of the Major Robert Rogers legend are found in the books. Legends involving daring and disastrous encounters between man and nature were delivered to readers also. Various aspects of the widely told Nancy legend of the White Mountains were collected by travel writers. Nancy was frozen to death in 1778 while trying to follow a deserting lover in a snowstorm, and there were those who believed they heard the shrieks and groans of Nancy's restless ghost on quiet nights. Collecting and repeating such legends formed an important part of the travel book. A reader might find a string of such legends as he turned the pages of a travel and descriptive book. For example, near Lake George, stage drivers pointed out the tree where Jane McCrea had been murdered by Indians, and travel writers acknowledged that such spots and traditions were appropriately lovely and sad. The western travel and descriptive writer James Hall collected many legends in his frontier travels, and he published them subsequently in a separate volume which enjoyed a wide popularity, *The Wilderness and the War Path* (1846). The folklore materials collected by travel writers range from a common motif in which a lake was said to have 365 islands, one for every day of the year, to more subtle and original items; one finds snatches of animal folklore belief, ghost tales, and myths like that of the Great American Desert.

Local color material was consciously gathered. The songs of the Minorcans at St. Augustine, the voyageurs, and the blacks, were collected. Robert Carter on his trip along the coast of New England commemorated the songs of the sailors. In *Forest Life and Forest Trees* (1851), a book which its author labeled wild and uncultivated like the forest, John S. Springer gave his readers the words of an original rum song which he had heard loggers singing. Previously published poetry by amateurs, collected in the course of researching a book, was inserted into books by travel writers also.

Minor folk heroes were portrayed by travel writers. Usually these men are variations of the Cooper hero Natty Bumppo. One reads of men without education who hunted for a living, were very strong, and had a kind heart. They usually were considered great hunters and certain marksmen. Writers reported that already legends were forming around this or that hero. These men were in complete rapport with forest life, might have killed a large number of Indians, might not be reluctant to give a rigmarole narrative of their adventures, and usually had wives and children. Charles Lanman told of one such folk hero who was an illiterate man; when asked to give an opinion of President Polk, said he had never met the state's governor because when the governor had visited his part of the woods years before, he had been off shooting deer " 'tother side of the ridge." Sounding a great deal like Natty Bumppo, a travel writer's folk hero might climb a peak and look down on all creation. What was lacking in these sketches and vignettes was the deep moral significance of Cooper's art and imagination. Thus, these passages written by travel writers are incipient literature, a sort of reservoir or mirror of cultural values, perhaps both.

Hunter folk heroes were compared to Daniel Boone, and in addition to the elements described above we find travel writers tapping the interest in violent adventure found in Indian narratives and in dime novels. There were exploits involving hairbreadth escapes, fights with wolves or panthers or bears, tales of a hero's adaptability to nature and his extreme individualism and self-reliance. Ethan Allen Crawford, who lived in the White Mountains, was an example of the tug of war between man and nature. He wrestled bears and fought wild cats. He knew all the woodcraft tricks of the frontier folk hero. Unconsciously uniting the American folk hero to the patterns of Old World mythology in order to secure a sense of newness and a sense of stability—that is, in order to reconcile the conflicts in the American mind—Crawford was said to possess a magic wolf fetter similar to the one the elves of Scandinavian mythology possessed. John H. Spaulding reported that Crawford once caught a wildcat with a birch withe. The folk heroes which travel writers put into their books generally lived the courageous primitive life of the hunter-gatherer. They were simple and frank. They are somewhat similar to the Natty Bumppo–Daniel Boone type, who reconciled the culture's concern for man's adjustment with the forces of nature to the philosophy of primitive nature.

In trying to put literary associations into the American scene, travel and descriptive writers reflected the American belief that the country lacked sufficient literary traditions, and by using the available body of popular American writing and adding materials collected in their travels they created associations which might reassure the national uneasiness about what were believed inadequacies. At times the young culture created new associations and embellished old ones. Thomas Starr King embodied the antebellum concern for historical

associations in a very provocative way when he described
Mount Hayes as clamped to a valley by two immense ledges
of bare, jagged rock, two miles apart, and looking "like the
carved paws of a colossal lion in repose." The desolate crest
of Mount Hayes soared over the valley "like a bald eagle's
head and beak," sat like a monstrous griffin overlooking the
village close by, and commanded a view of the river for twenty
miles. In ancient mythology the griffin guarded hidden treasures; and it seemed to antebellum travel writers that American
nature fulfilled admirably the symbolism of the griffin's form.
Travel writers gave Americans an important psychological re-
lease when a book of travel and description could make less
glaring the contradictory inclinations in their national character—when primitive nature could stand for newness and tradition at the same time, when the national mind could find a
way to reach a stand-off, when the national portrait was stabil-
ized and balanced.

~~~~~~

5

POINT OF REFERENCE

~~~~~~

The testing ground for discovering whether or not American culture had developed postures which insured stability and a clear sense of identity was the West. Travel and descriptive writers performed several cultural functions during the westering movement. Because there was much to know about the physical nature of the West and an eagerness to learn of the progress of civilization there, descriptions of the frontiers were always welcomed. Of course, between the lines of the reports there was more than practical information. Reports about the planting and transmission of culture westward gave assurances of the bright prospects of the country, of the maintenance of law and order, and of the rooting of institutions which would insure a unity between the new and old sections of the United States. Writers promoted confidence in the belief that American civilization would persist on the frontier. Once again, equilibrium was doggedly sought after, balance between wanted change and anarchy. With a fairly precise understanding of the role which their books might play, travel writers emphasized the need for a sure method of transmitting institutions westward. It was believed that a continuity of ideas, goals, and efforts which formed the national character resulted from literature and other labors of the mind. Writers warned fellow citizens obliquely that the Indian was doomed to extinction because his methods of cultural transmission were weak. They told readers about innumerable ties which bound Americans together as a culture and insured the survival of American civilization in the West.

Useful information for those planning to go westward consisted of medical information, climatic data, maps, and general descriptions, and it was provided at a low cost by travel books. Writers usually presented their readers with suggestions regarding the various ways to move west. The immigrant was cautioned as to his expenses while traveling, as to the important items to be sent by freight and the ones to leave behind, and as to the best season to travel to a specific location. He was warned against the injurious effects of new kinds of foods, of exposure, of overexertion while traveling, and of Indian rascality.

Traveling west on a steamboat involved risks. The danger of a boiler blowing up was ever present. But, in *Ensign, Bridgman, Fanning's Lake and River Guide* (1856) other dangers were called to the traveler's attention, One had to beware of gamblers. They formed a formidable and well-organized army on steamboats. Marked cards, loaded dice, and fraudulent faro boxes were the stock in trade of these men. The traveler had to be wary of the variety of methods used to suck him into a game.

Beyond issuing warnings and serving readers in practical ways, travel writers used their books as advertisements for western opportunities. Guidebook writers especially assisted the immigrant in choosing his new home, directed him to it, and through the promotional tone of his book gave the reader encouragement and made him feel part of a whole, unified national enterprise.

The books were also written to appeal to the easterner or southerner who stayed home, the businessman concerned about investment opportunities in the West, and the religious and civic-minded individual interested in seeing American culture transferred westward. Writers wanted to extract a favorable opinion for the West from the more civilized East, to stimulate interest in western natural resources, and to encourage religious and other cultural agencies of the older states to go westward. Travel writers implied that the study of the western character was the best perch for seeing the national character as it was tested and grew. Through a kind of comparative sociology within the culture, the cultural self could control what it was becoming and know what it was. Readers were told that any intelligent citizen would want to know well the geography, spiritual and material resources, and cultural institutions of every section of his country. The implication in such remarks was that the frontier did indeed have civilizing institutions or was well on its way to acquiring them. At the beginning of his widely read book, John C. Frémont made a knowledge of the West an essential national duty, because, as he noted, the immense region attracted the national mind and because the West was so enmeshed with important national concerns.

    In part, travel writers fostered and chronicled the transfer of culture westward. This chronicling role resulted from a clearly voiced concern in the East about civilized conditions in the West.* The isolation of western life might cause the inhabitants of the region to lapse into barbarism. Some reports pictured westerners living violent and uncivilized lives. Travel writers found Mississippi woodcutters who were free from all civilized control, looking only to provide themselves with food and shelter and to survive the harshness of primitive nature. Such types in travel literature were described as uncouth and unnatural. James Pattie observed that men in the wilderness were bound by little but a naked self-interest. It was reported that some pioneers went west to escape the law and too many had vagrant inclinations. Anarchic, uncouth, and restless types were given credit for setting the tone of western society. They were prone to heavy drinking, soured in temper

---

*Louis B. Wright in *Culture on the Moving Frontier* discusses the concern of the "parent hive" for the newly formed communities in the West (p. 35).

often, and bristling for a fight. Rifles, revolvers, or bowie
knives were ever ready. Law was yet a matter of prophecy in
the California mining area. Travel writers made such reports
throughout the first half of the nineteenth century, and it was
not only on the far western frontier but also on the Illinois
frontier in 1841 where barbaric and anarchic behavior was
found. The reports of these conditions threatened the parent
culture's, the East's, stability and the future prospects of the
whole civilization. It certainly threatened to make the national
character too shifting to define.

Frank reports were offset by more optimistic appraisals.
Travel writers emphasized the continuity of culture by finding
a check to lawlessness on the frontiers in the habits and
inherent capacities for creating and sustaining law which
settlers carried with them. A single spark of law, it was maintained, would check disorder. As a result, many writers of
travel and descriptive books not only reported the existence
of frontier barbarism, they wrote of the spontaneous development of social order from anarchic elements. This national
experience was turned around into more valuable a lesson
than all the gold found in California or the lead found in the
Midwest. Although there was a continual fear that law and
order would break down on the frontier, making one's pile
had to be buttressed by the law; this assured that the design
of the traditional culture would be perpetuated on the frontier.

Travel writers admitted that Americans in the wilderness
isolated from society often underwent transformations. These
Americans sometimes were unable to handle simple amenities
and social detail or lapsed into ignorance and gave themselves
up to the lowest animal instincts. But travel writers saw such
developments as warnings. Western life in some phases might
endanger much of the knowledge man had acquired over
many centuries, but there was never a sense of hopelessness
about the situation; rather, writers told easterners and western
settlers exactly what was in danger of being lost. Man in an
uncivilized state always moved toward a state of annihilation.
Barbarism was a miserable state, an uncertain, destitute,

gloomy, dreary, unhappy, and ignorant state of life, which
hindered rapid propagation and even survival. Travel writers
expressed in this attitude the culture's fear of impermanence
—not of time flowing in shifting cultural patterns but of
erratic, haphazard time which the human mind finds destructive. Colonial Americans had faced the same fear and needs.
Time is forever in flux for the American, who, disburdened
from a consciousness of the past and foreseeing perpetual
growth and development, often devotes himself to immediacy
and to culturally destructive or paradoxical patterns of
existence.

Travel writers countered reports of barbarism on the
frontier by using the it's-getting-better statement to describe
western society, and there was an effort to create the impression that the West was refined. Writers asserted that no
person would be treated uncivilly while traveling westward
if he behaved in a gentlemanly way. The antebellum American
was expected to believe the national character in the West
was not a backwoods type, nor heathen. Westerners were not
robbers, fighters, and gougers. Emigrant guidebooks endorsed
Illinois, Minnesota, and other sections as not being beyond
the pale of civilization. There were better classes in the West,
and they were not uneducated and unrefined provincials. The
half-horse and half-alligator types had disappeared some time
earlier. They had withdrawn beyond the frontiers and lived
in the imagination of reporters who confused a few wild
boatmen with the honest Christian settler. The American mind
tended to fear failures on the moral plane more than those on
the intellectual or cultural, while at one and the same time it
admired the wildness and freedom of the Mike Finks.

Western social refinements were cried up by writers, and
discussion of the rough edges was often avoided. Writers wrote
of ignoring the multitude of singular and uncouth phrases and
words called characteristically western, because they were
unworthy of notice. A few books even went so far as to claim
that the West was a model of refinement for the East. John
Peck asserted that throughout the West there were neighbor-

hoods and clusters of intelligence and refinement equal to any in the East. To prove beyond a doubt the gentility of the West, Daniel Curtiss claimed it was not unusual to find young ladies dressing flowers, pruning shrubbery, and cultivating a flower garden in which they took walks with their sweethearts. This propaganda for western fastidiousness was intended in part to convince cultural agencies, such as the American Tract Society and the Home Missionary Society, of their effectiveness in the West, as well as to attract settlers.

Travel writers in trying to stay the eastern fear that life on the frontier led to the breakdown of civilization voiced a concern similar to that of William Byrd of Westover in 1728. While surveying the boundary line between Virginia and North Carolina, Byrd was disturbed because the North Carolina frontiersman had shed the important vestiges of Anglo-Saxon culture—Protestant piety, protection of rights under law, good manners, and the spirit of enterprise. The antebellum easterner had the same concerns, and the rapid transfer of culture westward during continental expansion is one of the major accomplishments of the parent culture. Although the bellicose activities of the Mike Finks often demanded more literary notice, the prosaic job completed by another group of Americans was not overlooked by travel and descriptive writers. De Crèvecoeur had observed on the frontier an impure part of the people acting as precursors of the more enterprising. Travel writers, like their fellow Americans, were drawn both to the pure and impure and blended them into the national character.

One of the tasks of travel writing, especially of the guidebook, was to convince the East that the perpetuation of cultural values was a moral, religious, and profitable duty. Of course, it was understood that western immigrants had to take the initiative in this perpetuation, and the survival of institutions could result only from their actions, but travel writers also understood how cultural agencies and traditions work. Furthermore, an eastern and western cultural partnership in transferring civilization westward was believed to foster national unity. Elisa Steele visited a log cabin in the wilderness and observed the books the settlers owned, adding a few tracts to them and promising herself in the future to carry a few good books to give to these reading people. To the antebellum mind, a reading people were a civilized people. Books in this case contained the symbols of national belief to be preserved.

Travel literature reports suggest easterners wanted to hear what specific institutions were being transferred westward to assure the continuity of culture. Immigrants were exhorted to go westward with their Bible and eastern civilization and make a mark on the country there. Travels stressed the development of educational, literary, and religious institutions in the West. Final chapters of western travel books list almost every cultural agency on the frontier—lyceums, geological institutes, atheneums, etc. Writers implied that eastern social and cultural values were on the whole the ones the West admired and wanted for itself. This cultural behavior is remarkably similar to that found in the East where the progress of American civilization was sometimes measured against European standards.

First and foremost, travel writers emphasized the rapid development of western educational facilities. They understood the hardships of pioneers and the traditional role of schools and churches on the frontier as precursors of a stable culture. The antebellum ethos considered rough churches and schools as germ cells which insured the triumph of the organizing power of civilization. Civilization from this standpoint organizes reality and makes it coherent and comprehensible. Travelers were, thus, anxious to announce the advance of education westward. They told Americans at every turn that the blessings of civilized educational institutions were being formed, and that such institutions fostered law and liberty. These educational facilities were called transcendent. Every legislature in the West was said to appreciate the need to foster education, and easterners were told that few westerners were unable to read and write. Much money was being spent, and even colleges and seminaries of learning were rapidly arising.

Travel writers advised immigrants, after securing their survival, to acquire cultural institutions as rapidly as possible. Especially did the emigrant guidebook writers caution their readers about their duty to the whole country of which they were part. Pioneers were told to oppose violence, introduce courts, schools, churches, beneficial societies at the earliest possible moment. The pioneers were to pave the cultural path for millions yet to come. It is not surprising then to find that the boom town of Leavenworth, Kansas, four years after its founding, had a lyceum, tax-supported schools, lecture halls, dramatic entertainments, a bookstore, and a French restaurant. The transfer of civilization as evidenced by the progress of religious and benevolent societies was a preoccupation of travel writers describing the West. As early as 1849 wealthy citizens of San Francisco had formed a benevolent institution. Such institutions were described as evidence of western refinement and culture. No doubt some of these institutions were raw, judging by the experience of Mrs. Kirkland and others. Mrs. Kirkland chided the Montacute Female Beneficient Society for being the town's prime dissipation, an unexpansive clique, and a source of town gossip. Perhaps many benevolent and literary societies degenerated into sewing and gossip clubs. Yet such groups were as important for what they aimed to do as for what they failed to accomplish, and there are indications in the remarks of travel writers that the cultural institutions of the West contributed in some measure to the expansion of the intellect, the imagination, and humane sensibilities. It cannot be denied that reports of the flowering of culture on the frontier were discordant. Next to descriptions of developing cultural refinements in the West one must put the humorous accounts of an unpolished and sometimes very raw society. One finds descriptions of dramatic performances in the West which made the actions of the Duke and King in *Huckleberry Finn* quite believable. Some writers exaggerated the effects of western cultural institutions, others decried their weaknesses, but all suggest that the culture in delineating the national character encouraged specific goals which were to be achieved.

The role of prosaic cultural agencies in the transfer of civilization westward did not escape the attention of travel writers. Even a regular mail was considered a civilizing influence. The importance of newspapers as cultural agents was acknowledged also. Long lists of newspapers were included in travel literature, sometimes with indications as to their political leanings. A newspaper made a town, and it was held that American liberties were perpetuated through an independent press. The editor of a newspaper was a man to be admired because of what he could do for the country. E. S. Seymour eulogized the power of the press for diffusing light in the sparsely settled West; the press, for guidebook writers, had the unlimited power to be a blessing or a curse, of elevating or debasing the national mind. Newspapers were in the forefront of civilization on the frontier; as the compositor set his type, the Indian stared at the white man's mysterious ways. Listings of newspapers and other prosaic institutions were made by travel writers as evidence of western progress in the direction of eastern standards.

The force which all cultural institutions represented was used by travel writers as an instrument for defining the national character, but what was more important, it was believed that the West would influence the destinies of the United States. Therefore, the question was not only one of perpetuation, but also one of being aware of a unified nationalizing effect which common cultural values and institutions made possible. Travel writers found innumerable ties which bound the whole culture together as a people and extended over a vast country—ties which involved natural family relations, friendships, and duties to the nation's and God's laws. The culture's values encouraged a belief in its wholeness in the face of its sectional and social diversity and the vastness of its land mass.

In the attempt by travel writers to define and comprehend

the developing national character, the western character was measured against vague conceptions of American values. Theoretically at least, the West afforded opportunities for social and cultural innovations, modifications, adaptations, if not outright revolutions. Descriptions of lapses into barbarism demonstrate the nature of some changes, but what mattered most was an anxiety over which way the culture might jump, East and West, toward unity or anarchy.

Attempts to define the western character in travel writing gave the whole culture a chance to look at a part of itself, a part which was considered the prototype of the future American. Travel writers described seminomadic first settlers. To some these seemed an idle and shiftless people, know-nothings. The writers also found themselves on other occasions among the most intelligent middle class people, the bone and sinew of a country. This bone and sinew of the culture dealt harshly with the hunter-gatherer or idle, shiftless type in the reality of their everyday lives, although in their imaginative lives, their mythic lives, they endowed him with heroic proportions.

Travel writers attempted to categorize the variety of elements one might find in the western character. There were Hoosiers, Wolverines, suckers to be considered; frontier hunters were labeled *sui generis* in every respect, even in language. Westerners had nervous expressions and startlingly bold phrases. The East for them was called a tolerable frog pasture. Thomas Addison Richards in his *American Scenery* penetrated the deeper significance of western language and bolstered the myth of staunch western individualism while explaining its roots and nature. His use of comic exaggeration no doubt comforted all antebellum Americans, as it was the expression of untamed exuberance, an important index of the national self. In the description which follows, the idiom of humor was used by Richards to provide a sense of security and continuity for the culture; Americans used dark, wild laughter to cope with the fearsomeness of a harsh wilderness and of an uncertain identity.

You may take it for granted that a man who talks to you about using the forks of the road for a bootjack, won't submit to be kicked very patiently; and he who whips his weight in wild cats, and dodges chain lightning, will at least try to accomplish what he undertakes. He who has a soul as big as a courthouse, may very safely be trusted; and there is genuine piety in the breast of the old hunter, who economizes time by begging every Sunday morning that Heaven will bless 'its earthly table bounties and crittur kumforts, throughout the week!' I like the veteran who, when asked if he was not afraid of the rattlesnakes, numerous in this vicinity, nonchalantly answered, that he generally 'slept over 'em'; and the gallant captain, too, who when racing with an opposition boat, sits on the safety valve to keep it down with his weight; or, who when the watch cries out 'man overboard!' asks if he paid his passage, and being answered in the affirmative, sings 'all right—go ahead!' I do not think that such a man, who, though he can sail his boat on a wet blanket, or in the morning dew, would hesitate to launch out into deep waters.

The extravagances and optimism of western character were especially apparent on the gold mining frontier. Prosperity often led to an exotic expansiveness. The extraordinary abundance of gold and the easiness with which fortunes were made led westerners to lay down money without talk; the art of moneymaking was a petty concern to them. For some writers, this was a refreshing direction which the culture was taking; it displayed an indifference for moneymaking while still going after it. Americans could pursue money with a romantic flourish. Miners who struck it rich suddenly behaved as princes and philanthropists; rough, old sailors, hard-working Irishmen, and steady foresters from wild Missouri were suddenly sybarites.

Openness and familiarity followed these social conditions. Westerners moved about greatly and switched occupations often. There was a fiery energy in the western character which was necessary to accomplish what was being attempted, to make one's pile and make it quickly. The major asset of western character was described as a bold and self-reliant spirit. No one apologized overly for the evils which existed, because the energetic spirit was so very appealing. Westerners made decisions and acted upon them quickly. They understood the practical, egalitarian character of their society. The laborer was as bold and independent in his inner being as a merchant and landholder. Men living in ease and refinement did not know how the national character was modified by the need to expend energies settling a country, contending with dangers and evils in the wilderness, and engaging in the founding of the arts of civilization. Men who performed these feats had to be hardy, firm, free, independent, and generous. The western character thus described in travel literature reflected the imperatives of the age of the common man which assured every man his opportunity to be as upright and rich as his neighbor. The West was the great testing ground for this imperative.

Westerners were described as idiosyncratic in dress, sincere, and open. Western man outwardly seemed as gnarled as his oaks, but he was brave, strong, and humane; he occasionally trod as though he were lord of the prairies wearing a large diamond stickpin. He was not afraid of man or beast. He was ready for any emergency, boundlessly hospitable and well mannered. The westerner who spent his leisure time in a tavern was not to be faulted. There he learned manliness and quickness. He learned to talk sharply, quickly, and boldly. He studied human nature, not in books, but firsthand in life. This type of description by travel writers implied that the mythic American lived in the West and that the Andrew Jackson–Natty Bumppo hero had primitive, not civilized, spiritual roots. The West had its rowdies, as did the East, but there was another class at taverns in each town who exemplified how the national character was being shaped in the West.

Western man's character, travel writers held, was shaped by having to prove himself. Writers recorded anecdotes about strong men and good fighters who were nevertheless gentlemen, not bullies.

Western boldness and dignity were frequently recorded. Antebellum Americans were asked to believe that the West's moral exterior was as rugged and tough as the bison, but its soul was large and rich as the vast prairies. Although one might laugh at the extravagant expressions of the Westerner, their lawless hyperbole nevertheless contained a deep moral meaning, indicating through its roughness, strength and action. The western man was pictured as active, daring, and exuberant, honest and independent. He was an egalitarian who extended his philosophy to women. The curricula of western female seminaries included in travel books were meant to bear testimony to the fact. The Female Eclectic Institute of Davenport, Iowa, taught its young ladies bookkeeping, history, drawing, science, and mathematics.

On one hand, the American yearned for cultural uniformity and tried to fit the westerner into the national portrait; on the other hand, the westerner was considered unique, a new figure, a figure of innocence, a figure of the wilderness, a fantastic mythic force. The culture as a whole was looking at itself in the midst of the process it worshiped and identified as the American system—continual and persistently fresh change. In trying to delineate the western character, travel writers revealed the ambiguity which was created by a fundamental ambivalence toward the national self. Writers believed that in essentials the emerging western character was not so very different from the national character in the Atlantic states. There were only shades of differences created by the circumstances of western life. Members of the culture were told that the distinguishing characteristics—a spirit of adventurous enterprise, independence of thought and action, and an apparent roughness—were differences of degree only. After all, the West, as had been the case in the Atlantic states for so long, was a place where the best people could expect to live in a humble cabin for a long time without refinements or outward signs of social gradations. These circumstances led westerners to a sense of equality, a simplicity of manners, an independence of spirit, and freedom of speech. The pathway to a continuing national character in this case was realized through a western moral self.

The materialistic side of the western character was uncovered by the scrutinization of the immigrant's motives for going west. The first thing travel writers emphasized about

these motives was that the American went to better himself;
material success was consistently a dominating issue. Guidebook writers asserted that, while in the older states thousands
struggled to barely survive from year to year, by going west and
working hard these same Americans could secure an easy
living and often a fortune. Using the utopian-like propaganda
which colonial travel writers had used, antebellum writers told
their readers there were no beggars in the West and that
industrious men received credit. It was difficult for any westerner to believe that a newcomer had not come westward to
make his pile. Travel writers met men who asked them if they
had come west because they failed in business and wanted to
make good in a new place. Many travel writers announced
outright at the beginning of their books that they were writing
for those seeking fortunes in the West. Everyone had a chance
to become a millionaire.

Travel writers found it difficult not to exaggerate the opportunities for success in the West. If the West were the preserve of the purest elements in the national character, how
could a healthy, wide-awake man fail to prosper or even
make a fortune? Of course, reports of failure and a few
pessimistic predictions appeared in travel literature; however,
there had always been occasions for disillusionment in the
West, and self-pitying types were to be left alone to make out
for themselves. Pessimism was heresy in America; and even
James Pattie, broken by his western ventures, at the end of
his narrative spoke of weaving a new web of hopes. The
developing definition of the national character would not
support pessimistic reports, especially from its source of hope,
the West. Furthermore, failure was the individual's burden
in America; failure meant one was unable to live up to his
opportunities. The source of failure was not in the West or
the American system, but in the individual.

If writers of travel books generally agreed upon the cer-
tainty of success for the industrious immigrant, they were also
unified and vocal in saying agriculture was the best way to his
fortune. This agrarian perspective is reflected throughout

travel books. The first and greatest source of national wealth and the perpetuation of that wealth was to be derived from a hard-working, independent, agrarian people. Agriculture was called the lifeblood of the human race. The West in the schema was called the Garden of the World. In that garden the immigrant was to find the realization of the culture's highest hopes. Thus, the West and America were designed for an agricultural people. Farming was the basis for acquiring wealth, and the richest culture would be the one which would support the largest number of farmers. Rich, fertile soil undergirded the nation's glory, and thus, travel writers painted idyllic pictures of industrious, literate, skillful, and happy farmers. This portraiture gave the culture a middle group between a culture which lapsed into the hunter-gatherer stage on the one hand and on the other hand moved toward industry, commerce, and technology, which were lumped frequently under the term "internal improvements" by travel writers.

It is not surprising then to find writers telling readers to grow corn, not dig for gold, to buy a farm and get away from the crowded city. It was believed mining would give way to farming, and men of all professions would leave the older states to become farmers, supporting their families with ease and realizing inner contentment and harmony. All these descriptions of western pastoral life had the ring of Crèvecoeur's ideal American farmer.

There is a contradictory side to this agrarian self-portraiture in antebellum travel writing. It was reported that young men were attracted by both the industrial town and the West. Admitting that the United States was first and foremost an agricultural nation, writers nevertheless had to admit that manufacturing drew a continually increasing number of people to its ranks. It is interesting to find, in the travel writing which dealt with the West, a strong allegiance to commercial and industrial pursuits as well as to an agricultural life. Henry Nash Smith has shown in his *Virgin Land* that the West was seen by some Americans in terms of agrarianism and by others in terms of industrialism and commercialism. The mass mind harbored, paradoxically, both positions. While there was a vociferous dedication to an agrarian society, a considerable portion of travel literature was devoted to the praise of commercial and industrial pursuits.

Guidebook writers boosted frontier manufactures. Lists of mills along with notations regarding their technological sophistication, inventories of resources for industrial ventures, and catalogs of banking houses, commercial instruments, etc., filled sizable parts of travel books. Travel writers wanted it to be known that much activity involving nonagricultural pursuits was part of western life. In Illinois copper speculation attracted immigrants and men familiar in Wall Street. Although Morrell Heald has shown that the frontier acted as a refuge from advancing technology for many, travel books suggest that at the same time the West was also oriented toward acquiring the accoutrements of commerce and industrialism which signified progress in the culture.

The industrial and commercial interests and patterns of antebellum life penetrated the frontier along with the agricultural. Manufacturers were listed among the five or six classes of people who filled the Mississippi valley. In *Edwards' Great West and Her Commercial Metropolis* (1860) one finds illustrations devoted to industrial buildings of the West. Given an effective protective tariff, it was predicted San Francisco would become what she was destined to be—a great manufacturing city, the Manchester and Birmingham combined of the Pacific. The "Golden Gate" was considered a fit epithet for the portal to the commerce of the Pacific. In 1846 John C. Frémont awakened his readers to the Oregon trade's value; after all, Oregon had an excellent location on the north Pacific which faced Asia, it produced many of the goods of commerce, it enjoyed a mild and healthful climate, and it must become the great thoroughfare for the East India and China trade. Though preferring agricultural interests and fearing the dangers of business, travel writers admitted immense fortunes could be made in commerce. When Chicago surpassed Bangor, Maine, in the production of lumber manufactures, the event was proudly noted. All this is to say that writers underlined the antebellum double allegiance to an agrarian ideal and a growing commitment to the benefits of an industrial and commercial society.*

L. W. Hastings underscored this double allegiance by predicting a strange future for the agricultural society. He spoke of a Boston, a New York, a Philadelphia, or a Baltimore springing up rapidly in Oregon and California with a large population and all the amenities of civilized life. There were to be churches, magnificent buildings, spacious schools, and stupendous monuments, all in the Greek style, and overlooking the bustle and tumult of this civilization the great American mountains were to tower. Guidebook writers did not expect Lowells to spring up instantly, but they observed that the city had only to keep pace with the country and great urban centers would be built. The extensive granite resources of California were seen as the makings for great cities. The great prairies were to be overrun with cities and towns also. In a scheme to create a modern Athens in Texas, George W. Kendall projected colleges, squares, city halls, penitentiaries, public walks, public houses, and carriages running along the streets of a humming and thriving city. Westerners living in the midst of a lonely frontier did not anticipate the problems of cities; they found it impossible not to dream of clusters of happy people enjoying the country's material bounty. The mass was less misanthropic than its hero Daniel Boone.

In tabulating the choices of occupations westerners were presented with, travel writers attempted to harmonize the major values of the culture. According to O. G. Steele and other writers, the westerner could choose from opportunities in agriculture, commerce, or manufacturing. Travel writers proposed that the nation's wealth and health would be fostered by the harmonious hand-in-hand work of the agricultural and

*See Arthur A. Ekirch, *Man and Nature in America,* for an antebellum statement by Henry C. Carey who wondered if America should not attempt to diversify its life by achieving harmony between agriculture and industrialism (p. 37).

artisan populations. Industrialism and farming were to join forces, and both were accepted by antebellum mass culture if we judge from travel literature. Guidebooks were written for the farmer, the mechanic, and the capitalist.* The destiny of the West described by travel writers included the farm and the mill.

The interest in agriculture and industrialism was frequently expressed in an interesting admixture. Travel writers predicted the loss of the primitive character of western places and the cropping up of bustling Yankee towns. They described scenery but they also noted mineral resources for manufacturing and commercial growth. The reports sent eastward included a close scrutiny of mineral treasures, abundant water power, and inviting areas for manufacturing as well as agriculture.

The admixture of devotion to industrialism and agriculture takes on an interesting configuration when one looks at the travel writers' opinions regarding the railroad's function in the West. These opinions form a configuration in which the railroad, the machine, and the farm, the garden, work in tandem. The railroad was to serve both the farm and industry, and add to the national prosperity. Writers could see the impetuous locomotive leading eventually to harmonious gardens. Locations were designated as suitable for building great manufacturing cities if water power and the railroad had a chance to play a role. The railroad and telegraph were seen as unifiers of the country, not only in sentiment but in enterprise. Railroads and canals would insure broad western gardens. Technological developments were rushed to make western farmers healthy and secure.

In the final analysis, whether it was to be an industrial, an agricultural, or a joint agrarian-industrial future awaiting the westerner and the whole United States, travel writers decided the frontier symbolized promise. The West was to be the seat

---

*See Arthur K. Moore, *The Frontier Mind,* p. 139, for a discussion of the promise which the West symbolized; and on the same point Michael Chevalier, p. 313.

of virtue for the culture, free from the taint of effeteness and degeneracy, and western men in travel literature became a noble race embodying honesty, intelligence, and chivalry. Also, the valley of the Mississippi produced the largest race of men. This promise which the West embodied and symbolized for antebellum America was part of the traditional destiny American civilization envisioned for itself. This promise was expressed in epical terms. Great movements of populations carrying the threads of civilization to new places had a mystic quality to them. In such cultural postures assumed in travel writing, we discover the stance of Cotton Mather's introductory remarks to the *Magnalia Christi Americana* and de Crèvecoeur's "What is an American?" The American position was prophetic. Most travel writers wrote in terms of great future national glory. By including glory as part of the national destiny, travel and descriptive writers may seem to have merged incongruously idealism and materialism, but they worked out paradoxical patterns fundamental to the national character.

As presented in travel literature, the West believed it held the nation's destiny in its hands. Its reality was manageable, although the management required some tricks of logic to reconcile the paradoxes which developed as America approached its reality. The West and the United States were believed to furnish inspiration for great material and moral achievements. Travel writers fitted the West into America's messianic role, and for the mass mind they made complex cultural visions, as well as constructs mythic and less difficult to deal with. Thus, the tales of western immigrants became more marvelous than anything since Robinson Crusoe, Captain Cook, and John Ledyard; the earlier colonial experience was reenacted. The westering crusades were said to equal the expeditions of the Middle Ages in magnitude. This idea stirred the national mind and helped formulate the national self-portrait. Travelers westward considered themselves more or less heroes, and travel writers were swept up by this sense of heroism. They felt part of the establishment of the Empire of the West, a final link which would bind the world in enterprise. New clusters of value, modifications of heritage, formulation of new processes, and the development of new cultural constructs were in the offing. All these changes did not threaten the older culture; they were blended into a cultural design which made for a less precise national character, a national character less precise than western civilization had ever seen. Western destiny and the national destiny were woven into a mystical union with the land. Westerners lived amidst greatness, lofty mountains, large inland seas, immense forests and prairies, and imposing rivers. In this milieu physical nature would elevate the American mind. It would shape and create a national character which would nobly fulfill the culture's dream of producing true greatness in man. The West was a test— an opportunity to find ways to continue the American dream process.

6

A UNIFIED CULTURAL SELF

The culture's vision of the American as a "new man" ne-cessitated a unified definition of the national character. All the major elements had somehow to be brought together into a whole and labeled. Therefore, travel writing consisted of mov-ing toward that whole by giving readers a thoroughgoing self-analysis, a taking stock of national virtues and vices. Through these appraisals writers created collective self-portraits which reveal the contours of antebellum civilization, but the crux of the national character emerges also. However, to begin with, the writers were aware of the difficulty of generalizing about a complex, half-formed, pluralistic, geographically large, agrar-ian society that faced the beginnings of an Industrial Revolu-tion. After extensively scrutinizing American civilization, travel writers concluded that there was no country about which it was so difficult to generalize. One was confronted with im-mense diversities of tone and direction, of strength and adapta-bility, of sectional prejudice and individual beliefs which were created by life on the prairies, in the marketplace, on the southern plantation, in the small rural village, in the woods and mountains of the West, and in the eastern manufacturing city. Americans, it was agreed, shared common characteristics, but the national character seemed far from uniform. The country had to settle down and let the dust settle before a clear vision appeared of a homogeneous population held together by an entire national character. Whether one accepts the construct of national character or not, it should be noted that antebellum Americans did.

Travel commentators found their culture one-sided, irregular, and awkward; frontier life especially underlined this irregularity and awkwardness in American life. On the deck of a steamboat bound for California one noticed various types of Americans, including squatters, blacklegs, (professional gamblers), Mississippians, Arkansans, and a new variety of the American species. This new variety was tall, loose-jointed, larged-limbed, awkward looking, and dressed eccentrically. The face was long, sallow, covered with straggly black hair, and wearing a melancholy expression. The mouth and lips suggested a destructive nature. The new American chewed tobacco incessantly and lounged at length on the deck when he was not in the forward saloon taking drinks. He was well armed and expressed defiance of foreigners.

Each section of the United States was believed to have been shaped by differing circumstances, although amalgamation of sectional differences into a national character, it was granted, happened through intermarriage and cultural interaction. Travel writers wrote about a national character which was distinct in distinct sections of the United States, but this solution often led to vague national portraits. The writers usually had to rely on a definition of the national character in terms of an Anglo-Saxon heritage modified by the American experience.

The Anglo-Saxon element which travel writers consistently listed as a major unifying index of culture is the *spirit of enterprise,* and continually this spirit of enterprise was connected to material advancement. Enterprise as a cultural ideal became the principal determinant in the search for a unified national self. In a geographically broad country with seemingly unlimited resources, the spirit of enterprise was considered the unifying link of culture, not only uniting but also perpetuating the culture. Enterprise was believed to be the culture's major pathway to identity. Travel writers declared only active and brave individuals immigrated and carried civilization into the wilderness as Americans had from the very beginning of their history. The West best illustrated the truth of this self-conception. Westerners, like colonial Americans, were trained to enterprise from early life. Especially did western travel accounts reinforce the belief in and supply the evidence for the enterprising spirit as the key aspect of the American character.

Despite admissions of a diversity of cultural elements in the society, travel writers seized on a few ideas, like the spirit of enterprise, to extract from their observations a stabilizing force for the culture, a coherent identity. Enterprise, first of all, gave the culture a focal point for its identity which explained the flux resulting from rapid change and the formlessness created by a more or less traditionless society. The spirit of enterprise explained the chaotic present in the name of a better future. American history was always to be, therefore, in the future tense. The search for the New Zion in Puritan America had a similar pattern and, therefore, contributed a kind of continuing force to an idea which the Industrial Revolution transformed for its own purposes.

By using the spirit of enterprise as a unifying element for the national character, American hyperactivism was given a rationale. Americans understood travel writers who boasted about the activist spirit which penetrated into every cranny of the world with its trading and trafficking. This activism, it was reported, produced few scholars, but Americans could be consoled to have fewer peasants and beggars also. The intense activism was also vividly apparent in reports of hotel and boarding house life. These residences were so regulated as to permit a short time for meals and exhibited a lifestyle suited to active pursuits. A bell sounded, a meal was eaten in minutes, and then people scattered to their separate occupations. British travelers objected to this life in their books, but Americans had no time for leisurely chats with autocrats over tea cups. Americans were on the way to twentieth-century automats.

The very air of the American environment was described as being pregnant with a magnetic kind of bold enterprise. The society seemed like a dizzying whirlpool with no time for thought. Everything was done at breakneck speed, travel writers reported. Time was in the objective case for Americans. Travel writers believed Americans lived in a fast age. Their lives were ordered on a high-pressure steam principle. Everything was done with a go-ahead spirit. Christopher C. Andrews wrote of a man who upon asking if a toll for a bridge covered the return trip learned that everything was go ahead in this country. Travel writers found Americans too busy with business and unwilling to give time to strangers, but it was nevertheless high praise to have a guidebook call the people of this or that town a driving people. American hurly-burly activism shoved the travel writers about, but their complaints were gentle and patient. Writers reported all sides of American hyperactivism, the nervous expressions and daring of pioneers, the rambling and speed-loving character of pleasure travelers, but the reports suggests energy was highly valued.

Travel writers tried to encourage Americans to use their energies in a nondestructive manner, however. Restless energy resembled the turbulent steam locomotive, and the speed of locomotives and the pressure of steam led to derailments and explosions. Excesses were feared. Intense exaggeration must not become part of the national character. The motion or activity with which Americans stamped their identity also created anxiety. For while activism was appropriate in the business sphere, it became ludicrous in a social one, and it was inimical to serenity. Americans wanted to be happy as well as rich. Travel writers encouraged Americans to imitate Europeans who enjoyed their recreation fully and did not carry into it their tensions and excesses, the hurry and fury, which dominated American business and social life.

The spirit of enterprise was part of a long-standing work ethic in American culture. Travel writers consistently described the country as one in which all must work. The

American accepted willingly the primal curse, he deified work, and would have commended Adam's sin as a sound principle. Labor had a high value. Work was reported as a prescribed way of life. Any man who chose to ignore this ethos exposed himself to censure and gossip; a travel writer in the course of his exploration might find it difficult to find a man of leisure as a companion in many American cities.

An additional part of the enterprise–hard work syndrome, as seen in travel writing, emphasized the belief that hard work insured material success. The spirit of enterprise was to lead the American to a fortune. What came after the fortune frequently proved bizarre. Americans continued to seek prosperity even when prosperous, and if they had bad luck some perversely wished for worse luck, because they looked forward to a full delight when good luck inevitably came. Americans never allowed themselves to be disappointed. The *action* only had to continue to satisfy the national mind. In such attitudes one finds a double-edged, dark, self-boosting operating; as at so many other points in American history, myth became more important than reality, underscoring an old habit of using myth as a pathway to individual and cultural identity. One finds such patterns in travel writing as well as in *The House of the Seven Gables, Redburn, Leaves of Grass,* and *Walden*. Ninety-nine out of a hundred young Americans, it was believed, were determined to be rich, and for the American mind this attitude gave birth to industriousness, frugality, ingenuity, perseverance, and ultimately inner and outer success; for while a man made his fortune, he made himself.

The latter belief contains an inherent archetypal life process. The get-ahead and go-ahead slogans of antebellum America merged into a mythic belief in continual movement and beginnings, which gave both culture and individual a reality always in the future and always exuberant and fanciful. This mythic aspect of American culture revealed itself on the high and popular culture levels. For Thoreau and Whitman the continual beginning expressed through images of the dawn and the cyclic process of life and death, was a spiritual process; for the frontier speculator in land, copper, or gold, the continual beginning, good or bad luck, was a material process. At least, it was a material process on the surface. The mass mind, however, often tried to merge the ideal and materialistic.

In trying to consummate this merger, the mass mind, as expressed in travel writing, tried to discriminate between getting rich as a ruling passion and getting rich as part of a grander individual and cultural scheme. Getting rich meant realizing specific New Zion dreams for the individual and for the whole society. One could not deny that the heavy emphasis on getting rich took a toll on the public taste and intellect, on the ability to make distinctions between right and wrong, and on the development of youthful minds, but these temporary defects did not preclude future triumphs of the mind. The money mania was to give way to the glory mania.

Travel writers found Americans willing to risk everything to achieve their immediate and ultimate objective. It was first things first, but great things were not neglected once survival was certain and prosperity at hand. The national character had to buy, sell, and gain. It had to concentrate its energies upon speculating and accumulating. Everyone had to throw the dice. In five years every man expected to be a nabob. Calm would come later, now was the time for all American men to become rich. Here there was no room for idlers. Travel writers found men speaking of what they could get out of the country, not what they would achieve. Before the nation could direct itself to noble energy, it had to achieve ease and wealth.

The intense desire for money and the use of money as a standard of success were analyzed by travel writers as part of the unfolding national character. The expression "It don't pay" was stamped on much of the metal in the national character. The accumulation of wealth was such a thoroughgoing concern in antebellum life that social standards and etiquette were geared to that concern. Hucksters invaded the gates of Greenwood cemetery. Commentators complained that rich children did not play with poor children. Servants, if Americans let themselves be called such, would not work for employers who did not maintain a rich enough display of wealth. Men and women were judged by the latest fashion in clothes which they wore. What a man spent made him respectable and respected. Americans spent money indecently and vulgarly, but there was no other way for a man to let other men know when the American dream of success had come true.

The role of travel writers was to chide gently the overcommitment to getting, to the practical, to business, and to suggest where the national character should put its energies once affluence arrived. There was a religious and poetic element in American life to be sought also. The urge to get should not degenerate into the loss of close familial ties, into a worship of veneering, into the buying of theatrical furniture, and into the supporting of idle women in barbaric splendor. It was understood that gross materialism and a naive vision of life eased a sense of rootlessness and impermanence which had ironically resulted from a dedication to material growth. The Americans had to be instructed by travel commentators in the art of living. The culture had to be taught to value a luxurious carpet not because it spoke with emphasis of twenty thousand a year but because it was beautiful and soothed the senses. In many respects, the prosaic symbols in travel writing were fully transcendental, and although the expression of ideas lacked artfulness, travel writers gave their readers emblems of materialism which pointed upwards.

Where the transcendentalist and popular travel writer parted company might be in the mass admiration of shrewdness and speculation. Luck as well as pluck was valued; writers showed that Americans admired a sharp deal and a man willing to risk, to swap, and to gamble. How glorious was the squatter who brought a martin box to a quarter-section and on the strength of it swore he had a house eighteen by twenty, leaving the buyer to presume the feet! How delightful the thought of a shrewd American finding the White House empty and preempting it! American children were said to have a disposition to trade or swap which began in childhood. The speculative spirit in the national character can be seen in the traveling game of prairie loo, which involved scoring the number of different wild animals seen en route, and the antebellum expression "going it blind." On the copper mining frontier the American intellect and emotion was so sheeted with copper that everyone was feverish, men, women, and children, about copper mining. The grand word which was the lever of all expression was "conglomerate." It was used to describe scenery and to relate everyday affairs. Children used it as an ejaculation! The southwestern humorists treated this exuberant side of the national character effectively in their books, and some humorists used the travel book style. Travel writers were codifying the national character, while the humorists with greater art probed the deeper meanings of the culture's patterns of life. However, some travel writers came very close to working both sides of the street. We find artful and symbolic accounts of the American propensity for gambling. For example, boys at a tender age risked a few pennies on some venture. If nothing else was available, they might bet on the name of the steamboat coming up the river, or which way the wind would blow tomorrow or maybe next week; a group of children might sit quietly around a table, each with a lump of sugar in front of him and each ready to take the stake if his was the first lump upon which a fly alighted. The latter was not an uncommon practice, and the description not untypical for travel writers.

The American concern for material success was often connected to another major index of the national character, egalitarianism. Everyone was to have an opportunity to make his pile. The individual American was informed that his institutions gave him as good a chance to get rich as they did his neighbor. Men believed firmly that they were the architects of their own fortunes. Every man had a stake in the country. Here, one could believe, everything was developing, changing, unestablished. There were no aristocracies, no primogenitures.

Character and fortune resulted from individual enterprise. By law, no classes had special privileges. America, unlike Europe, represented promise for everyone. The White House apartments were open and accessible to all citizens at levees. Social equality which existed everywhere without exception insured all travelers attention and care, regardless of rank at home; they had only to be well-mannered and good-natured, travel writers asserted.

Especially in the West one found a passionate regard for equality. Western men had a high sense of their personal worth. They very readily announced that they were nobody's servant but their own. A man who had been a gentleman of quality in the East felt no shame in driving hogs for an old settler. The West was the supreme test for the culture. It was labeled the most democratic country in the world, and one learned that it was shaped by a practical equality in which men who once had had professions dug cellars, drove ox teams, sawed wood, or carried luggage. Men who had done manual labor headed profitable establishments and frequently wielded political power. A man who considered another below him on account of his appearance or job would have trouble living peacefully in the West. Labor was respectable. The West achieved the Jeffersonian dream of a society where the natural aristocrats moved upward in the society and led. Men of all ranks were propelled into positions of leadership by the free and traditionless character of society. Travel writers in giving these reports were performing a sacramental function.

The democratic conditions of the West and the westerner's sense of his own worth produced minor ludicrous situations. During the Constitutional Convention in California, one member of the convention objected to the word "peers" in the phrase "tried by a jury of his peers." He reasoned that it was not republican; and he wanted to know what the United States wanted with peers, as it was no monarchy and had no parliament. The national character was expressed often in such free-of-the-past, arrogant, defiant, and fantastic tones.

In attempts to formulate a definition of the national

character, the Yankee image united with the major cultural indices of enterprise, activism, and egalitarianism. The United States was called the universal Yankee nation; and New England, considered the home of the Yankee, represented the cultural fountainhead for many of the indices of the national character. Among travel writers the Yankee figure played a key role in the search for cultural identity, and the source of the spirit of enterprise in the national character was usually traced to New England life and culture. Minnesota, for instance, was called the New England of the West because its geographical location and healthful climate were sure to foster industry and enterprise, and its water power resources, pine forests, and other advantages would encourage manufacturing. St. Louis, it was proclaimed, would become a city known for its New England character once it came under the influence of the tried American enterprise. Guidebook writers emphasized the role of New Englanders in transforming the wilderness. The many New England settlers of Missouri and Illinois brought with them sober and industrious habits for which the North was known. Thus, the presence of the Yankee in the West, at least according to travel literature, served as a cultural point of reference.

The Yankee character was an expanding and changing part of the reality of the Atlantic states and made defining the national identity somewhat easier, because the parent culture observed the outlines and features of its future, continuing self by studying its western offspring. The expanding and changing part of this national portrait permitted the culture to realize the working of its own mythic life process of perpetual beginning and change. It was a way of seeing the future in the present. There was an attempt on the part of the South to work out a similar cultural pattern of identity, but the South failed because it had weaker tools of cultural transmission and more importantly because its major myths negated the use of the most effective tools of creating a national identity in a developing industrial society — activism and materialism. Activism and materialism were the tools of the

Yankee. However, a role for the South had been formulated from the seventeenth to the nineteenth centuries which made it a buffer and foil for the central cultural design.

To compound the difficulties the South faced in terms of fitting into a unified national identity, southern life and activity were often defined with the northern fountainhead as a point of reference; for example, Georgia was described in travel literature as the Yankeeland of the South. Underlining the force of the Yankee spirit, one read about native New Englanders in the South, who, though away from home for years, maintained a strong spirit of enterprise. The implication of this statement was that the South might possibly corrode the spirit of enterprise. The widespread belief in the synonymity between the Yankee and restless activistic enterprise was raised to the mythic level in a delightful account by Grenville Mellen. New Englanders, according to Mellen, were, like Franklin, highly given to practical invention, and the greatest number of patents were awarded to New Englanders. The New Englander was reputed to be seldom without his pocket knife, which he used with dexterity; even New England boys at school were seen whittling a windmill or some other toy. So universal was this trait that a gentleman in Havana who gave a large dinner party was said to have supplied each man from New England with a shingle to cut in order to avoid having his furniture carved.

If the Yankee, né New Englander, symbolized American force and energy, industry and ingenuity, travel writers described the southerner in contrasting terms. First and foremost, the southern character made for cultural dissonance in terms of the spirit of enterprise. The typical view found the South backward materially and not working toward the material progress which was the hallmark of Yankee states. The greatest single condemnation leveled against the South was that she lacked the spirit of enterprise. This opprobrium did not generally depend on the sectional bent of travel writers.

If the South had had enough time it might have fitted itself into the national pattern of enterprise. Southerners like

John Esten Cooke did not retreat from the possibility of using Virginia's natural resources to foster the economic development of the South. William R. Taylor has shown in *Cavalier and Yankee* that a mythic South served the national psyche as a place of respite from materialistic striving, as a place of time, permanence, and tradition in a fluctuating, anchorless society. Travel writers sensed a need to accept the southern respite role and fit it somehow into the national character at the same time. Travel and descriptive writers perpetuated a long-standing stereotype of the southerner as lethargic and unenterprising. This stereotype seem to make the northern and southern ways of life irreconcilable. However, read in psychological terms, the South embodied many of the antebellum civilization's most cherished mythic values, and perhaps the Civil War coming at the end of the era was an attempt unconsciously by the culture to destroy ego ideals which were no longer serviceable culturally.

The South represented a parent culture, the agrarian colonial civilization, with which the culture had formerly as a whole identified and to which it gave allegiance in a philosophy of a primitive nature, in the literature of the historical romance, and in folklore. However, there came a point when the culture had to reject a part of itself—part of its reality. It had to destroy one part of itself which had been mythologized as its essence, that is, the simple and primitive ideal. The reality of primitive or, on a lesser plane, pastoral nature existed in the culture, but the culture chose to worship a fictional primitive-pastoral lifestyle rather than incorporate into the culture a hunter-gatherer way of life. Encouraging this cultural posture is the fact that the American is a romantic civilization. The South was considered the preserve of romantic values.

It is not surprising then that a divided cultural self was led to the melancholia and hysteria of war. The culture looked back at an idyllic childhood and faced the reality of adulthood. The culture, like Hamlet, was divided in itself and faced self-destruction. It is not only that the culture did not have

a precise identity, but that its identity was composed of antithetical elements which prevented it from meeting everyday
existence rationally. Like the neurotic living only in the past
and future, antebellum culture was psychologically divided
between two sides of its reality, the increasingly materialistic,
commercial, activistic side and the mythic and primitivistic
side.

The South was said to be out of step with the national
character in terms of activism. Some writers thought the
cause of this condition was inherent or traditional. Some
travel writers found the South in some instances moving backward toward barbarism. The criteria used to come to this
conclusion were unused natural resources, lack of material
growth, and the absence of technological progress. Too many
manufacturing facilities were going unused. Too few men
were engaged in manufacturing. There were too few tanneries,
sawmills, and textile mills. To compound the problem, Southerners were found to dislike northern activism and the Yankee
eagerness for change and progress. The Southerner found
satisfaction in all that was, displeasure in all that might result
from rapid change. Travel writers documented a lack of go-
getting and ingenuity, a lackadaisical attitude toward business
in the South. Some Southerners were declared destitute of all
enterprise.

Travel writers did not by any means create a black,
negative portrait of southern life. There was, as in all else
dealing with the national character, a great deal of ambivalence toward the southern character. In John Pendleton
Kennedy's *Swallow Barn*, Frank Meriwether, an example of
the southern character, was inclined to be lazy and philosophical. He had little mercantile interest, but the noncompeti-
tive side of the southern character was characterized both
positively and negatively for the mass mind. Southern character was both admired and decried. The Yankee side of the
national self envied the mythic southern gentleman self, but
the deification of work controlled the development of a unified
national character. Work was moral; therefore, no work, no

morality. The southerner, long committed to an illusion about himself growing from his environment and traditions, half-yearned for nineteenth-century technological power while he continued to pose as a pastoral figure in the national portrait. He has continued to this day to do so, in television as John Walton, for instance. In the search for a unified national identity, the role-playing of the southerner was precarious. He eventually was crushed by a frantic search for the national character. Radical social changes in the antebellum period resulted in a psychic trauma, an anxiety hysteria over the question of uniting the national self. The two-hundred-year calm of a fundamentally stable cultural life during the colonial period was suddenly being swept away in the maelstrom of industrial, commercial, transportation, migratory, and political revolutions.

Colonial values could not be discarded entirely; the United States was to remain essentially agrarian for some time. However, the American mind was plagued by the need for self-analysis and seeing into the future. The future was reality for Americans, and this fact makes it difficult for a culture to deal with its immediate reality. It is important to examine further the faulting of the southerner for embodying the essence of colonial life, that is, a slow and calm bucolic existence, because the pastoral golden age embodied by the colonial experience was the Jeffersonian dream to which many antebellum Americans gave allegiance. In probing the psychological side of the national character, southern life came closest to the general character of this dream and the South was both condemned and admired because of this circumstance. The whole culture faced two ways—in myth toward the peaceful old agrarian society with a primitivistic character, and in practice toward the activistic, new, commercial society. No doubt unconsciously the dangers to the American dream of justice and equality inherent in the Industrial Revolution were a cultural concern. No doubt the national mind was reluctant to face those new, fearsome pressures.

The South bore the heaviest burden of our national paradoxes. This fact becomes evident when one encounters dis-
cussions of southern lethargy in travel writing. A pattern of
frustrating contradictions and tensions very subtly led to the
Civil War. A civil war, thus, existed in the national character
before 1861; and the South by being given a paradoxical
mythic role materialized the psychic conflict of the culture.
The Civil War was one brutal way to choose, unconsciously,
industrialism, materialism, and activism and reject the Jeffersonian static vision of a calm, bucolic life commingled with
an unmolested primitive nature. At some point the ideal in
the American dream was equated with unleashing the tech-
nological-energy syndrome. The Civil War settled the matter
emphatically.

The ambivalence and psychologically tortuous nature of
these processes are apparent in the assumptions made about
southern character. Writers theorized that enterprise, intelligence, and virtue were more generally present in people who
lived in northern climates than in those in southern. They
wrote about the disrepute of labor, the lack of egalitarianism,
and the existence of slavery as impediments to southern
growth. Pleasure-seeking idleness was traced from colonial
times downward, especially the rather-starve-than-work attitude. Southerners reportedly thought trade and labor vulgar.
Such stereotypes conflicted with the major indices of activism
and enterprise declared as matrices of the national character.
The South was pictured as feudal-like, rejecting the culture's
tenet of egalitarianism. A northern teacher might be welcome
into a southern home to teach, but she was not admitted on
an equal basis to southern society. Of course, many writers
held that slavery unpropitiously modified southern character.
It paralyzed enterprise and enfeebled industry. It prevented
the development of manufacturing. It sometimes encouraged
the lowest barbarism. In any event, indolence was a hallmark
of southern life. A southerner killed time without giving it a
thought. Intellectually he was not inquisitive, because he was
constitutionally lazy and retrogressive. In such remarks the

positive-cavalier-myth side of the southern character was ignored momentarily. Contradictory emphasis about southern life made the Civil War inevitable.

In the South poor farming methods were described as standard. Manufacturing efforts were doomed by the fact that the laboring class was degraded and inefficient. The South lacked an interest in education and had a disrespect for intellectual pursuits, according to the travel book stereotype. The contrasting dedication to education by the Yankee was heavily underlined; and the fact that the South was behind the North and West in educational facilities and literacy was forcibly stated. Southerners did not miss what northerners considered the everyday essentials of civilized life. This was a typical attitude. A widespread belief expressed by travel writers held that ignorance was very prevalent in the South. It was not surprising, then, to have introduced a southerner who thought a piano a great wonder and another who spoke of the biblical town of Babby Lion. Even writers with southern backgrounds granted the intellectual state of the masses in the South was low, because of the lack of schools and few opportunities for social intercourse.

The Southerner suffered a reputation for being in an inferior position vis-à-vis the predominant national achievements. Writers of books for the pleasure traveler declared a close description of much of the South would be uninteresting and unimportant to their readers. Invidious comparisons between southern and northern scenery, climate, cemeteries, and spas appeared in travel books. Travel writers wrote of places in the South where a plow was almost unknown or a moldboard on a plow a novelty. The Georgia cracker was ignorant, improvident, lazy, and narrow-minded, but the Cape Codder was intelligent, discreet, and expansive intellectually. Both were frank, bold, and simple, but clearly the Cape Codder had the edge. Although these alleged flaws prevented the development of a unified national identity, there were ways a travel writer might balance them against positive values to encourage a reconciliation and a sense of unity in the American mind.

Analyses of the national character juxtaposed to the negative southern portraits a southern lifestyle which had an assuring, quiet, feudal-like glow. If the southerner contradicted the belief in enterprise and material progress on one hand, on the other his way of life preserved the American Eden and gave the activist-materialist side of the national character an opportunity to pause and consider the American system from a different internal perspective. Both the South and West acted as foils for the central self. The South acted as antebellum America's psychic refuge from the forces of industrial society, and from this standpoint the South was treated positively. The South and North might differ in thought, feeling and opinion; but the southerner was described by travel writers as proud, dignified, epicurean in the best sense, generous, high-minded, hospitable, a lover of the outdoors and of sport, and a gallant quick to fight a duel.

Cotton and sugar planters might be known for their indolence, quick temper, and dissipation, but they were also high-minded and had a spontaneous sense of humor. Joseph H. Ingraham found young Mississippians less inclined to dissipation and more honorable than young men in other states. They were not the irascible, hotheaded, and quarrelsome creatures they were so often reported to be. They were warmhearted and generous, seldom beaux or effete bucks, dressing quite plainly. Some travel writers found all recklessness in the South, but many found this recklessness delightfully infectious. Southern wildness, not unlike western wildness, was at times paradoxically juxtaposed to the nonactivist stereotype of the southerner. This characteristic wildness was not so unlike American activism in general. In friendly descriptions, southerners became gallant, high-spirited, lofty, lazy beings, free from crass and petty moneymaking inclinations; again one is reminded of the free-spending, expansive western character. Travel writers objected to the nonegalitarian love of titles in the southerner, but the epithets used to describe his habits of

hard drinking, gambling, horseracing, cockfighting, and tobacco chewing suggest admiration and envy for the mythic
cavalier tradition of the southern character.

Thus, Americans reading travel books not infrequently
heard of intelligent, expansive, cordial, and dignified southerners. Travel writers reported that the best southern society
branded slavery evil. It was not untypical to find plantation
owners being given the romantic pastoral treatment. In this
treatment, plantation masters were descended from old chevalier stock and enjoyed a secluded, luxurious country life.
There were none of the stratagems of modern, metropolitan,
commercial life among them. Such statements show that the
travel writers looked to the South as the seat of chivalric,
ancient traditions, that is, for a sense of time and permanence.
At the opera in New York the travel commentator was struck
by the superior air given to the men of the audience because
a large number of southern gentlemen were present. Southerners given the leisure to gain a full stature and a mind not
overburdened with responsibilities and business had style, a
dignified bearing. It was hoped the North might cultivate this
novelty and perpetuate it in the national character.

The travel book southerner disdained the Yankee and
was dismayed by the Yankee invasion of the South. Writers
found it necessary to claim the term "Yankee" was an honorable, not a reproachful one. Travel writers wrote of being
asked if they were a Yankee or a white man. Southerners were
said to think of all Yankees as peddlers. The Yankee businessman was disliked in the South; there were too many unwanted
invasions by northern managers and products. It was probably
even more galling to read about factories established in the
South successfully run by Yankees. Southerners might be said
to scorn Yankees, but travel writers hint that Southerners
hoped to catch up technologically and industrially to the
North. Writers let it be known that the South had been fully
awakened to the importance of railroads. Unrivaled resources
for prosperity and wealth were beginning to be developed. In
some cases, there were reports of the spirit of enterprise

among southerners. The South had bright prospects; Georgia had the enterprising character of a northern state. Travel writers reported hopeful developments. Southern cotton factories would condense the population, and then labor and education would acquire dignity. The South could look forward to all the benefits of civilization. The result could only serve to unify the national character. The dignity of labor, education properly valued, and material prosperity were emblematic of freedom and individualism.

In defining the national character, travel writers had to position minorities in their cultural self-portraits. They did this by determining in what way and to what degree minorities assented to or dissented from major cultural indices. Thus, Shakers, Mormons, the Irish, the Germans, the French-Canadian, the Mexican, the Negro, the Indian, and others were examined in terms of the extent to which they encroached upon American cultural goals and especially by how they measured up to the spirit of enterprise. After learning of the Mormon church's richness and the hardworking and prosperous condition of the Mormons, the travel writer found room enough for all this strange group for a long time. Pleasure travelers in their frequent trips to Shaker settlements found an acceptable, hardworking people, and guidebook writers recommended tours of Shaker settlements. Social, religious, and sexual aberrations or eccentricities were permissible within the culture's enterprise, hard work–activism syndrome. The Irish were judged on the basis of their being good or bad workers. In the South, if an Irishman broke his back there was no loss, but an injured Negro meant a loss of labor and money. The German-Americans were often praised for their good work attitudes.

Creoles in New Orleans were described as less enterprising and ambitious than Yankees there. The Mexican was evaluated on the basis of how he measured up to Yankee activism and enterprise. When the Mexican did not adopt the system of his Anglo-Saxon neighbor, he was morally, physically, and intellectually outdistanced in the grand race of progress.

Mexicans clung to old customs, were inherently indolent, and rejected change; in the age of progress and steam, they were doomed. The American industrial and agricultural systems were trumpeted as being superior to those of almost all minority groups. The American people's spirit of enterprise proved itself formidable and insurmountable at each instance when it met a subculture which departed from the activism-enterprise syndrome. American culture was certain to triumph and become the dominant culture; travel books assured Americans of that fact. Within the framework of self-congratulations when comparing themselves to minorities, Americans filled in the outlines of the national identity, and their security was enhanced by knowing not only what they were not as a culture, but by knowing that what they were insured them cultural survival, prosperity, and dominance.

Mexican mines could not operate properly unless under the direction of an enterprising Yankee, and southern cotton mills succeeded better under Yankee control. Wherever industrious Yankee activity was lacking, there were poverty, no manufactures, and a culture which produced little of value. French civilization in the southwestern United States could not match the accomplishments of the American system of free, civilized, Christian republicanism, because its feudal system was not expansive or progressive. Judging them in terms of American enterprise, the writers found French-Canadian farmers near Detroit, though amiable, characteristically ignorant and unambitious. Other minorities suffered similar condemnations in travel books.

The black man, often stereotyped as careless and contented, a jovial and childlike individual, fell under the American-enterprise standard of appraisal. Some writers granted that the black man's dullness, lack of enterprise, and inefficiency were due to slavery and admitted that when his self-interest was involved he worked hard, but the more widespread view among travel writers was that the black man was naturally lazy. Admitting that slavery was an evil, John Lee Williams wanted only enterprising Americans to bring their

miraculous order, system, and economy to Florida to demonstrate that they could do more in one day than a slave could
in a week. Travel writers frequently described the black man
as a poor laborer.

As Americans searched for a unified sense of cultural
identity, they were faced with the realization that in their
midst Indian civilizations were being rapidly destroyed. Although romantic and sentimental views of the Indian existed
in the culture, travel commentators consistently declared that
Indian civilization undermined fundamental American cultural drives. Indian standards differed, especially, in the area
of the spirit of enterprise. The Indian was condemned time
after time for his indolence and ignorance, and for travel
writers he symbolized a barbaric obstacle to the white culture's survival and perpetuation. As the Indian did not adapt
to the activist culture and persisted in his lazy ways, his destruction was pronounced inevitable.

The image of the noble savage was a cherished literary
asset, but travel writers were nearly unanimous in their belief
that the Indian was doomed. There was often an epical and
sentimental, as well as harsh, tone to this pronouncement.
Either the white man or the Indian would be forced from the
land. The Indian had to submit to his destiny and vanish. If he
and the bison refused the burden of labor, they had to perish.
According to some writers, the red man preferred extermina-
tion to removal westward. Like the buffalo, beaver, elk, the
Indian was disappearing before the march of civilization, and
travel writers could not tell which would become extinct first.
Many travel writers found Indian life rigidly fixed and beyond
improvement.

What travel writers described was an Indian unwilling to
play the part of the activist enterprising Yankee—to work and
try to accumulate wealth. Travel writers with puritanical fervor
declared the real Indian was unlike the creations of Cooper
or Longfellow. The Indian did little credit to humanity; he was
considered a slave to his animal appetites and especially to sloth.
He had to die out to make room for God's chosen people who

would subdue and cultivate the earth.

Thoreau also read the Indian's destiny in terms of extinction. It seems at first glance startling to find that the culture which set up a hunter-gatherer, Natty Bumppo, as an epic hero in its mythology could destroy the types in reality; however, the literary Natty in truth supplanted a white reality which was disappearing, and Cooper himself saw the type as doomed. What we had, then, was a young culture putting into its imaginative life something which would soon be unrealizable in its real life. Although the imaginative was part of the real life, when the imaginative conflicted with rather than supported the other side of that life, the culture moved toward inner division and self-destruction. The nature of the culture's response to these conflicts depended on the individual strength of its two parts, the physical and the imaginative. If the physical existence had more value in the culture, then a physical attempt would be made to unify the culture's self-image. If the imaginative was stronger, then the reverse became necessary. If the two elements were in balance, the tension in the culture would persist.

In discussing the Indian's fate by contrasting him to the black man, travel writers embodied a configuration of antebellum attitudes toward the black man, the Indian, and the white American self, and indirectly embodied the culture's deep conflicts. Charles Fenno Hoffman's comments stand as typical:

Providence seems to have designed that this mysterious race should not continue upon the earth; and fate has infused a fatal thirst into their bosoms, which is hastening their doom with fearful celerity. But six years ago, and the woods around me were alive with Indians; now they are only traversed by a few such stragglers as these. You may talk of civilizing them—but that, too, is impossible. You may more easily civilize the stupidest African than the most intelligent Indian; and yet, who for a moment would compare the erect port and manly tread, the air, the *blooded* look of the one, with his keen sagacity and rare instincts, to the misshapen form, the shuffling gait, the stupid bearing of the other? Where, then, lies the difficulty?—the African is an imitative animal, and the Indian is not. He will copy the form of your weapons, for he has felt their edge; and he will make himself rediculous by wearing a cocked-hat, because he conceives it to be an emblem of authority. Rings and bracelets he may wear, for they recommend him to his tribe; but the forms and fashions of civilization he despises. The negro furnishes the best raw material for a dandy that can be had; he learns at once how to wear his hat and adjusts his shirt-collar according to the last mode of the white man. The Indian, if a fop, departs even farther than usual from the costume of a European. He comes from Nature's hands all that she ever intended him to be—the wild man of the woods. To the fleetness of the deer traversing the forest, he united the instinct of the hound in finding his way; and when you add to these the mental gift of a certain wild eloquence, wholly unimprovable by cultivation, you have nearly summed up the intellectual qualification of the American savage—the genuine child of Nation—the untamed—the untameable.

A great deal is unconsciously revealed in Hoffman's statement. His analysis contains the force of the Puritan's view concerning American culture's life and destiny. His description also contains a revealing attraction to the doomed Indian. In some ways the Indian symbolized the essence of the first American experience with the continent—the primitive experience. The Indian was proud and determined, heroically accepting annihilation because of an unshakable belief in self; at the same time the Indian resisted acculturation into the so-called superior culture. In travel and descriptive books Indians were shown exhibiting the self-respect and independence which was crucial to the white national character—and ancillary to the elements of enterprise and egalitarianism. The Indian both attracted and repulsed Americans. Observe the reasons for the demeaning position of the black man in Hoffman. The Indian was the subject for tragedy, i.e., he was to be taken seriously; the black man was a subject for comedy, i.e., to be laughed at. This viewpoint demonstrated a joy in acknowledging the Indian as the genuine child of nature, because antebellum Americans partly defined themselves in such primitivistic terms. They found in the Indian an historical and fraternal identity. Annihilate the Indian, and the fraternity had to be established in the culture's imaginative life. Behind these cultural postures a psychic self-murder led to a recurring controversy about the real Indian in nineteenth-century literary criticism. The confusion in the controversy was caused by not seeing that what was being sought was not the real Indian, but the real unified national self.

7

CONFIGURATION

Travel and descriptive writers gave their fellow Americans a unified national character which they hoped would pull together all the clusters of values, sectional characteristics, and minority dissonances. They were trying to do in a brief historical time what takes much longer periods in cultural matters. Henry James said it took a great deal of history to make just a bit of literature. So too does it take a great deal of common experience for a culture to reach the point where its national identity is so taken for granted that there is no need to define it. There is no need for an un-American activities committee. But emergence of American proverbs, prayers, sacramental functions, and time associations created clusters only. A catalyst had to be introduced to make the culture whole. Identifying matrices was not enough for travel writers either.

In trying to describe and explain the national character to themselves and to Europeans, travel writers invariably tried to resolve uncertainties and contradictions, to unify their conception of the national life and character through the concept of promise or destiny. The style they chose to give this explanation was epical, lofty, and spacious like American scenery. In analyses of the national character, writers came to the summing up with a sense of prophesy, and American destiny was prophesied in apocalyptic terms. This view of the national character was romantic and idealistic. Americans did not pride themselves on their past, but on what they expected to be. Like the heir to a great empire, they claimed respect. Americans were laying foundations for future civilizations the likes of which had never been seen; and they were doing this with a spirit of enterprise superior to the one which built Carthage and Ilium. John Gregory declared that America, very shortly, would produce a race of men perfect in terms of intellectual and physical ability, surpassing any people of ancient or modern times. The spirit of Whitman's "Passage to India" pervades travel and descriptive books.

Foreigners were unable to look beyond American rawness and see the promise the young culture stood for. Travel writers explained how the nation was temporarily concerned with materialistic striving and practical ends. The American commercial spirit might be anathematized by travel commenators, but with all its flaws commerce was a step forward in a march of human progress, a step which would eventually encircle the world with a gold band of brotherhood. The clusters of technology joined to hard work, primitive nature as sustenance, and individual self-reliance, led in one direction, the direction of promise. Travel writers and other Americans persuaded themselves to reject the records of the past, to focus on subduing the continent, to use nature and manufacturing jointly, to build roads and ships in the belief that all American life led to some utopian end. Eventually this temporary destiny or folkway of practical materialism became an irresistible way of life; the means too often completely overshadowed the ends.

The antebellum American had no crystal ball. He believed foreign critics judged his culture by a home standard and did not give the United States credit for its accomplishment and promise. It puzzled American travel commentators that foreign travel writers did not see the close connection between national promise and a materialistic commitment to secure the greatest good for as many citizens as possible, to free men from drudgery through technology. The end of labor for the American was to do away with labor. A temporary dedication to a work ethic was acceptable when one foresaw a future utopia. Both present and future were bright. Travel writers encouraged readers to think of themselves as a people who began early to work and think for themselves, who believed in the here and now as a pathway to the future and to a completed identity. Americans could by using their wills and opportunities satisfy their wants and desires, cultivate their talents, affirm their individuality, and become models of manliness and womanliness. In the antebellum mind, the national character was pointed toward an earthly kingdom for the great mass of Americans and in the grand summarizing view the United States would someday gain a prosperity never seen before on such an extensive scale and baffling all predictions. There would be no need to ask where to after the millennium was reached. A culture, like an individual mind, finds ways to get around the difficult obstacles of reality.

Descriptions of the national character were frank, perceptive, and mythic. Travel writers explained their culture and its prospects well. They could not help but do so, because they were expressing their prejudices, and as André Gide suggested, civilization is a collection of prejudices. What we have seen is civilization using a collection of prejudices to deal with reality and self. There was no reason for travel writers to omit outrageous national characteristics caused by active, materialistic striving, as they ultimately fitted into the schema of the culture and were cloaked by the term "promise." Travel writers, nevertheless, had no easy task. They had to cope with the culture's formlessness, its variety, and its contradictions. They had mythic tools and used them. For instance, the melodies of the black man became the national airs of America because their mock cadences well fitted the broad absurdity of the words; their reckless joy, irreverence, antagonism, and perseverance were declared expressions of the mass mind.

The travel writer united the mythical and the fabulous in a realistic view of himself. He was like the Hudson River steamboat *New World* covered with an obvious filigree framework of white wood and surmounted by a huge engine. The *New World* was an apt symbol for the national character. Travel writers knew that. It was as sleazy and outrageous as American manners and dress, and conspicuously practical. The American had a great head of steam on and might blow up anytime. He was sharp looking, heavy-handed, nervous, uncertain; yet he strutted in a bright-colored coat with gilt buttons, patent leather boots, and silk vest from which hung his metal emblems. The machinery of the steamboat *New World* was like the culture's working parts. The culture drove recklessly straight along, jarred the cut glass and fine mahogany in drawing rooms, and shivered the filigree to pieces. Antebellum American travel writers found this new world quite a pleasant place. They decided that their culture and the national character were intact and comprehensible.

As it was revealed in American travel writing, the national character consisted of divergent elements united by a vague construct. Descriptions of pleasure travel show citizens hurriedly moving about their country to study statistics and cemeteries, but really attempting to define themselves. We also see a nature aesthetic developed which had more to do with cultural consciousness than with aesthetics. Prosaic travel literature supplied the first mass culture with mythic patterns and postures to cover up its uncertainty about its reality and its identity. It also helped gloss over the culture's contradictions. The portrait which often emerged was jagged—containing haphazard strokes, clashes of colors, and black humor. For all their attempts to paint a national portrait that was symmetrical, the final product was very nearly surrealistic.

These jagged portraits, nevertheless, help us understand the persistent workings of American civilization, especially the process by which we deal with our conscious and unconscious realities. The national character which a collage of travel books yields contains interesting but very cluttered syndromes. It is not so important that the culture approached nature variously —as a national treasure, as a horrifying experience and threat, as something to be crassly manipulated, or as a route to self-

knowledge; what is important is that the culture tried to develop a posture and an overall cultural design with which to
live and organize conflicting values. One might argue that the
unified cultural self travel writers created is intellectually thin
and even hazy, not very substantial; but when one puts together
all the cultural props travel literature constructed, one is not
so much interested in the outlandish character of the edifice as
he is in the process, the cultural tool, and the result as compared to other expressions of intelligence the civilization produced.

The national character then was philosophically imprecise
as presented in travel and descriptive literature. Travel writers
draped the national mind with a gauzelike set of ideas about
itself, and the contours of the national character were evoked
by terms such as "promise," "grandeur," and "epical." To a
considerable extent, we continue to work with the same vision
of ourselves and our values today, because the national character developed the way it did and its definition was created as
it was in mass literature and elsewhere. Travel writing was a
forum for dissecting and transmitting American postures and
contains clues to our subconscious life as a culture. Thus, we
find that significant patterns of a culture's inner life can be
traced in a group of closely related literary materials, for mass
culture uses such materials to study itself, to define its conscious reality, to assuage its inner doubts, and to manipulate its
major constructs. In a way, travel books performed the work
of all art—to express intelligence, to deal with reality and experience. Ironically, American culture is a culture whose inner-
most direction is countercultural. In the antebellum period one
can trace the development and firming up of this cultural
locus. Colonial values collided with the Industrial Revolution,
and the resultant value was an emphasis on flux and energy as
well as on stability and serenity. The national character has
accommodated and continues to accommodate itself to para-
dox. It is directed by rootlessness and roots, by form and formlessness. Tocqueville understood our problems well. We were
to him a sort of throwback culture, put in a primitive life posi-

tion Western man had not experienced for hundreds of years; but we also dragged along our baggage of two thousand years of civilization, our cultural memory. Melville in *Redburn* observed that you could not spill American blood "without spilling the blood of the whole world," and Melville made the greatest use of the travel book genre. He used it from the beginning of his career to probe, to quest, call it what one chooses, but he went beyond the confines of ordinary reality to enter a world stripped, intense, and essential. He too was concerned in his own way with the national character, and he had questions similar in nature to those popular travel writers asked.

The origins of popular or mass culture are traceable to the eighteenth and nineteenth centuries; Professor Russel Nye holds that mass society was fully formed by the middle of the nineteenth century.* American civilization is, perhaps, the archetype of mass cultures. The development of mass art is linked to the growth of mass society's technological-industrial orientation and its nineteenth-century social and political reforms. American mass art is related to the essential element of nineteenth-century technological and social revolutions—numbers. The indices used to study mass art are the large number of its productions, the mass consumption of its productions, the endless repetition of similar or identical artistic patterns, and the variety of aesthetic values upon which it is based.

Mass art faces a number of hard questions. Is it committed to conventional and mass values? Is it predictable, unimaginative, and commercial? Is the popular artist one who crassly panders to the low taste of the masses? Does he merely corroborate the mass experience rather than probe and enrich it? And, if one grants that he merely corroborates the mass taste, is his corroboration capable of being intellectually satisfying or aesthetically beautiful—reaching beyond itself in a way? Does size of audience, or mass production, or mass diffusion, or the diversity of technological instruments used by the mass media require some special consideration in judging and inter-

---

*Russel B. Nye, *Notes on a Rationale for Popular Culture*, p. 4.

preting the accomplishments and meanings of mass art? When
do gimmicks become artistic tools, if ever? In terms of quality,
are there times when the lines between high and mass art are
blurred? Is a new aesthetics needed for judging popular arts?
Most importantly for this book, does mass art lead us to the
deeper significance of our realities?

We all have experienced mass art in one form or another,
and as members of a culture which produced it we share the
commond bond of experience which it creates. There is much
unseen and deep in the realm of mass art which cannot be dismissed. The traditional tools of criticism need to be joined to
the insights of psychology, sociology, anthropology, and multi-
disciplinary approaches to knowledge to probe the significance
of its patterns and themes. If one accepts Preserved Smith's
dictum that "literature may be considered as a long soliloquy
of the race talking about itself," we should be prepared with
Russel Nye to readily "erase the boundaries" which have long
divided the arts and explore more freely the "vast unknown
terrain of popular culture." We may as a result hear more
clearly our culture's soliloquy and understand more fully what
forces have partly shaped us for over a century.

This book was made to give readers a broader context from
which to judge the American literary and cultural heritage.
If the mass of travel and descriptive books reflect the values
and concerns of our culture, then they represent part of ourselves which cries for exploration—our values, conflicts, and
postures toward reality. Mass art expresses these cultural characteristics from its special vantage point.

Mass literature contains one part of the world which enor-
mous numbers of people have inhabited and relished for a long
time. Its literature might not be the world the elitist wants our
culture to relish and inhabit as tenaciously as it has, but rejecting its impact will not make it go away nor help us move
toward a total understanding of it and ourselves. It is important to know to what extent it does or does not contribute to
the development of our humanity. In making its impact upon
our consciousness, it has affected the way we deal with our

realities, as well as determined the kind of repressions and sublimations required of man as a cultural animal.

This book explored part of the world of mass literature, but it was intended to lead to a holistic study of literature and culture. Travel literature was written for and read by the masses; it was popular. Much of it had a long-standing relationship-impact on the culture, which became ingrained by repetition and by subtler ways into the national psyche in the form of new mythologies, new archetypes, and fundamental patterns of approaching our imaginative and "real" lives. The reader is encouraged to make as many radical juxtapositions as possible in trying to achieve a holistic approach to American culture and literature through this book.

Our full national experience includes patterns and themes buried in our mass literature. Stylistic ineptitude is not a serious enough problem to deter our exploration of this large part of American civilization. The understanding of our escapist dreams and our inept popular idioms may clarify the meaning of other parts of our cultural selves and therefore become useful in helping us deal with reality. In addition, millions of people fill their imaginative lives with mass art. This book has mapped out the territory and substratum of one part of American mass creativity—its drives, its limitations, and its fantasies.

Long ago Irwin Edman wrote that "art is another name for intelligence." Mass literature should be approached with this broad definition in hand, considering it from the standpoint of the concerns of human nature and the variety of expressions of human intelligence in a cultural setting. Mass culture has its own kind of intelligence, and this book dissected that intelligence as it explored, often in elemental ways, many aspects of what it believed or wanted to believe was reality. Without doubt, the dissection often yielded a montage, an impressionistic collection of patterns and cultural themes which need to be placed against other parts of the culture's artistic accomplishments. Perhaps, in the course of making these placements, the relationship between mass and high culture will become clearer, and one will discover that the fundamental relationship between the two is *life*. Once this relationship is grasped, the quality of mass literature may seem a little more significant than it once did and its deeper meanings will surface. Then Dana's description of an awesome iceberg, Holmes's use of an American boarding house as a setting for his autocrat, Poe's borrowings for his Pym, Emerson's search for the American character by traveling to Victorian England, and the travel genre element in Melville's quests for identity and value may be fitted into a national design of symbols. For mass travel writers expressed what major American writers have said about the American self. What is important about America and Americans is not substantive. It is not the vastness of her scenery which counts; America implies the idea behind vastness. Antebellum America helped create the cultural laws by which we are governed.

BIBLIOGRAPHY

Abbott, John S. C. *South and North, or, Impressions Received During a Trip to Cuba and the South.* New York, 1860.

Abels, Henry I. *Travellers' and Emigrants' Guide to Wisconsin and Iowa.* Philadelphia, 1838.

Adams, Henry. *History of the United States of America.* 9 vols. New York, 1962.

Adams, Percy G. *Travelers and Travel Liars 1660–1800.* Berkeley, 1962.

"American Principles." *Harper's,* 14 (February 1857): 409–14.

Andrews, Christopher C. *Minnesota and Dacota.* . . . Washington, D.C., 1857.

"Are We a Happy People?" *Harper's,* 14 (December 1856): 207–11.

Barber, John Warner, and Henry Howe. *Our Whole Country.* 2 vols. Cincinnati, 1863. This book was first published in 1861 and was based on four years of travel.

Bartram, William. *Travels* 1791.

Beecher, Henry Ward. *Star Papers, or, Experiences of Art and Nature.* New York, 1855.

Belden, E. Porter. *New York: Past, Present and Future.* New York, 1849.

Berger, Max. *The British Traveller in America 1836–1860.* New York, 1943.

Bird, Robert Montgomery. *The Hawks of Hawk Hollow*. London, 1856. First published 1835; dramatized 1841.

Boardman, Harvey. *A Complete and Accurate Guide to and around the White Mountains*. Boston, 1859.

[Bobo, William M.] *Glimpses of New York*. By a South Carolinian. Charleston, 1852.

Bohn's Handbook of Washington. Washington, 1852.

Bond, J. Wesley. *Minnesota and Its Resources*. . . . New York, 1853.

Bowen, Eli. *Rambles in the Path of the Steam-Horse*. Philadelphia, 1855.

Bowen, Lorenzo H. *Bowen's Picture of Boston*. Boston, 1833.

Bredeson, Robert C. "Landscape Descriptions in Nineteenth-Century American Travel Literature," *American Quarterly* (spring 1968): 86–94.

Brogan, D. W. *The American Character*. New York, 1944.

Bromwell, William. Off-Hand Sketches. *A Companion for the Tourist and Traveller over the Philadelphia, Pottsville and Reading Railroad, etc.* Philadelphia, 1854.

Bronson, Francis S. *Bronson's Travelers' Directory from New York to New Orleans*. New York, 1845.

Brooks, Van Wyck. *The World of Washington Irving*. New York, 1944.

Bryant, Edwin. *What I Saw in California: Being the Journal of a Tour . . . in the Years 1846, 1847*. New York, 1848.

Bryant, William Cullen. *Letters of a Traveller*. New York, 1851.

Byers, William N., and John H. Kellom. *A Hand Book to the Gold Fields of Nebraska and Kansas*. Chicago, 1859.

Byrd, William. *History of the Dividing Line*. 1841.

Carter, Robert. *A Summer Cruise*. Boston, 1865. This account of an antebellum trip appeared in the *New York Tribune* during the summer of 1858.

Catlin, George. *Letters and Notes on the Manners, Customs, and Conditions of the American Indians*. New York, 1842.

Chapin, William. *A Complete Reference Gazetteer of the United States of North America*. New York, 1843.

Chevalier, Michael. *Society, Manners, and Politics in the United States*. Ed. John W. Ward. New York, 1961. Based on the 1839 ed.

Child, Andrew. *Overland Route to California*. Milwaukee, 1852.

Child, Lydia Maria. *Letters from New York*. New York, 1843.

Cist, Charles. *Sketches and Statistics of Cincinnati in 1851*.

Clarke, Asa B. *Travels in Mexico and California*. Boston, 1852.

Cleaveland, Richard J. *A Narrative of Voyages and Commercial Enterprise*. [1842].

Clemens, Samuel L. *Huckleberry Finn*. 1884.

––––––. *Life on the Mississippi*. 1883.

Colton, J. H. *Colton's Traveler and Tourist Route Book through the United States of America and the Canadas*. New York, 1854.

Colton, Walter. *Deck and Port*. New York, 1850.

Conclin, George. *Book for All Travellers*. Cincinnati, 1855.

Cooke, John Esten. "Virginia: Past and Present," *Putnam's Monthly Magazine*, II (August 1853), 195–202.

Cooper, James Fenimore. *Notions of the Americans*. 2 vols. 1828.

––––––. *The Pathfinder*. 1840.

Cox, Ross. *Adventures on the Columbia River*. New York, 1832.

Crèvecoeur, Michel-Guillaume Jean de. *Letters from an American Farmer*. 1782.

Cumings, Samuel. *The Western Pilot*. Cincinnati, 1843. Many eds.

Curtis, George William. *Lotus-Eating: A Summer Book*. New York, 1854. First published 1852, consisting of letters written for the *New York Tribune*.

Curtiss, Daniel. *Western Portraiture, and Emigrant's Guide*. New York, 1852.

Dana, Charles Anderson, ed. *The United States Illustrated*. New York [1855].

Dana, Charles W. *The Garden of the World, or, the Great West, Its History, Its Wealth, Its Natural Advantages and Its Future.* Also, *A Complete Guide to Emigrants, with a Full Description of the Different Routes Westward.* By an Old Settler. Boston, 1856. Includes prospectus of the Vegetarian Settlement Company.

Darby, William, and Theodore Dwight. *A New Gazetteer of the United States of America.* New York, 1832.

Dare, Charles P. *Philadelphia, Wilmington, and Baltimore Railroad Guide.* Philadelphia [1856].

Davenport, Bishop. *A New Gazetteer, or Geographical Dictionary.* Philadelphia, 1838.

Davison, Gideon Miner. *The Traveller's Guide through the Middle and Northern States and the Provinces of Canada.* Saratoga, 1833. This book ran through many editions between 1825 and 1840.

Dearborn, Nathaniel. *Dearborn's Guide through Mount Auburn.* Boston, 1841.

Delano, Alonzo. *Life on the Plains and among the Diggins.* 1853. Rpt. 1936.

DeVoto, Bernard. *Mark Twain's America.* Cambridge, 1951.

Dickens, Charles. *American Notes.* 1842.

Disturnell, John. *Disturnell's Railway and Steamship Guide.* New York, 1853.

———. *The Emigrant's Guide to New Mexico, California, and Oregon.* New York, 1849.

———. *Springs, Water-Falls, Sea-Bathing Resorts, and Mountain Scenery of the United States and Canada.* New York, 1855.

Drake, Joseph Rodman. *The Culprit Fay and Other Poems.* 1835.

Dulles, Foster R. *Americans Abroad: Two Centuries of European Travel.* Ann Arbor, 1964.

Dwight, Theodore, Sr. *The Northern Traveler.* New York, 1826. Editions appeared in the 1830s; first published 1825.

Dwight, Theodore, Jr. *Summer Tours.* New York, 1847.

———. *Travel in America.* Glasgow, 1848.

Edman, Irwin. *Arts and the Man.* New York, 1939.

Edwards, Richard, and M. Hopewell. *Edwards' Great West and Her Commercial Metropolis.* St. Louis, 1860.

Ekirch, Arthur A. *Man and Nature in America*. New York, 1963.

Ellet, Mrs. Elizabeth. *Summer Rambles in the West*. New York, 1853.

Ensign, Bridgman, Fanning's Lake and River Guide. New York, 1856.

Fanning's Illustrated Gazetteer of the United States. New York, 1853.

Farnham, T. J. *Travels in the Great Western Prairies. . . .* [1839]. 2 vols. London, 1843.

Fay, Thomas C. *Charleston Directory and Stranger's Guide For 1840 and 1841*. Charleston, 1840.

Fisher, Marvin. "The Iconology of Industrialism, 1830–1860," *American Quarterly,* 13 (fall 1961): 347–64.

Fisher, Richard S. *A New and Complete Statistical Gazetteer of the United States of America*. New York, 1853.

Fishwick, Marshall. *Confessions of an Ex-Elitist*. Popular Culture Association, 1971.

[Flagg, Edmund]. *The Far-West, or, A Tour beyond the Mountains*. 2 vols. New York, 1838.

Flint, Timothy. *Recollections of the Last Ten Years . . . in the Valley of the Mississippi*. Boston, 1826.

Foster, Lillian. *Way-Side Glimpses, North and South*. New York, 1860. Travel letters dated 1853 to 1859.

Freeman, Samuel. *The Emigrant's Hand-Book and Guide to Wisconsin. . . .* Milwaukee, 1851.

Frémont, John C. *Narrative of the Exploring Expedition to the Rocky Mountains in the Year 1842, and to Oregon and North California in the Years 1843–44*. New York, 1846 (D. Appleton and Co. ed.).
————. *Geographical Memoir upon Upper California*. House of Representatives Document, miscellaneous #5, 30th Congress, 2nd session, January 2, 1849.

Fuller, Margaret. *Summer on the Lakes*. 1843.

Garrand, Lewis H. *Wah-to-Yah and the Taos Trail*. Norman, Oklahoma, 1955. First published 1850.

Gerhard, Frederick. *Illinois as It is. . . .* Chicago and Philadelphia, 1857.

Gilman, Caroline. *The Poetry of Travelling in the United States*. New York, 1838.

Gilpin, William. *The Central Gold Region*. . . . 1860.

Goodrich, Charles. *The Universal Traveller*. 1836.

Goodrich, Charles A. *Family Tourist*. Philadelphia, 1840.

Greeley, Horace. *An Overland Journey*. Ed. Charles T. Duncan. New York, 1964. Based on the 1860 ed.

[Greene, Asa]. *A Glance at New York*. 1837.

Greer, Ann L. "Early Development in America, 1825–1850, of Travel Books as Literature." Unpublished Ph.D. dissertation, University of Southern California, 1955.

Gregg, Josiah. *Commerce on the Prairies*. 2 vols. New York, 1962. Unabridged 1844 ed.

Gregory, John. *Industrial Resources of Wisconsin*. Milwaukee, 1855.

Grinnell, Josiah B. *Sketches of the West, or, the Home of the Badgers*. Milwaukee, 1847.

Hale, Edward E. *Kansas and Nebraska . . . An Account of the Emigrant Aid Companies, and Directions to Emigrants*. Boston, 1854.

Hall, Basil. *Travels in North America*. 1829.

Hall, James. *Letters from the West*. 1828.
————. *Statistics of the West*. Cincinnati, 1837.
————. *The Wilderness and the War Path*. New York, 1846.

Haskel, Daniel. *A Complete Descriptive and Statistical Gazetteer of the United States of America*. New York, 1843.

Hastings, L. W. *Emigrants' Guide to Oregon and California*. Cincinnati, 1845. Facsimile reproduction, 1932.

Hawthorne, Nathaniel. *The House of the Seven Gables*. 1851.

Hayward, John. *A Gazetteer of the United States of America*. Hartford, 1853.
————. *The New England Gazetteer*. Boston, 1839.

Hazard, Samuel, ed. *Hazard's United States Commercial and Statistical Register*. 6 vols. Philadelphia, 1840–42.

Hazard, W. P. *American Guide Book*. Philadelphia, 1846.

Headley, Joel. *The Adirondack, or, Life in the Woods*. New York, 1849.

Heald, Morrell, "Technology in American Culture," *Stetson University Bulletin,* 62 (October 1962): 1–18.

[Henderson, Charles G.] *A Hand-Book for the Stranger in Philadelphia.* Philadelphia, 1846.

Hoffman, Charles Fenno. *A Winter in the West.* 2 vols. New York, 1835.

Holley, O. L., ed. *Picturesque Tourist.* New York, 1844.

The Home Book of the Picturesque. New York, 1852. Facsimile ed. with introduction by Motley F. Deakin, 1967. Includes essays by Irving, Cooper, Henry T. Tuckerman, Bayard Taylor, and others.

Horn, Hosea B. *Horn's Overland Guide.* New York, 1852.

Howe, Henry. *The Great West.* New York, 1857.

Hutchings, James M. *Scenes of Wonder and Curiosity in California.* San Francisco, 1861.

Huth, Hans. *Nature and the American: Three Centuries of Changing Attitudes.* Berkeley, 1957.

Indiana Gazetteer, or, Topographical Dictionary. Indianapolis, 1833. Other later eds.

[Ingraham, Joseph H.] *The South-West. By a Yankee.* 2 vols. New York, 1835.

Irving, John Treat. *Indian Sketches.* 1835.

Irving, Washington. *A Tour on the Prairies.* Norman, Oklahoma, 1956. First published 1835.

Jefferson, Thomas. *Notes on the State of Virginia.* 1784.

Johnson, Overton, and William H. Winter. *Route across the Rocky Mountains . . . of the Emigration of 1843.* 1846, Rpt. 1932.

Johnson, Teho T. *Sights in the Gold Region, and Scenes by the Way.* 1849.

Jones, A. D. *Illinois and the West.* Boston, 1838.

Kansas Herald, Leavenworth, Kansas. *Emigrants' Guide to Pike's Peak.* Leavenworth, 1859.

Kendall, George Wilkins. *Narrative of the Texas Santa Fe Expedition.* 2 vols. London, 1844. Facsimile reproduction, 1935.

Kennedy, John Pendleton. *Swallow Barn.* Ed. W. S. Osborne, New York, 1962. Rpt. of 1853 ed.; first published 1832.

King, Thomas Starr. *White Hills*. Boston, 1859.

Kirkland, Caroline Mathilda. *A New Home, or, Life in the Clearings*. Ed. John Nerber, New York, 1953. First published 1839.

Knapp, Samuel Lorenzo. *Picturesque Beauties of the Hudson River and Its Vicinity*. New York, 1836.

Knauer, J. *Minnesota Territory: An Account of its Geography, Resources and Settlement*. New York, 1853.

Langworthy, Franklin. *Scenery of the Plains, Mountains and Mines*. Ogdensburg, N.Y., 1855.

Lanman, Charles. *Adventures in the Wilds of the United States*. 2 vols. London, 1859.

The Latter-Day Saints' Emigrant Guide. St. Louis, 1848.

Leonard, Zenas. *Narrative of the Adventures of Zenas Leonard*. Clearfield, Pa., 1834. Several eds.

Lewis, Alonzo. *The Picture of Nahant*. Lynn, Mass., 1855.

The Lightning Line. An Illustrated Guidebook. . . . Philadelphia, 1859.

Lloyd, W. Alvin. *Steamboat and Railroad Guide*. New Orleans, 1857.

Loomis, J. V. and Co. *The United States Statistical Directory, or, Merchants' and Travellers' Guide; with a Wholesale Business Directory of New York*. New York, 1847.

Lowell, James Russell. *Fireside Travels*. Boston, 1864. This book contains "A Moosehead Journal" (1857).

Lyford, W. G. *The Western Address Directory: Containing the Cards, etc., of Business Men in Pittsburgh, Wheeling, Zanesville, Portsmouth, Dayton, Cincinnati, Madison, Louisville, St. Louis; together with Historical, Topographical and Statistical Sketches for the Year 1837, etc. Intended as a Guide to Travellers. To which is added a list of the Steam-Boats on the Western Waters*. Baltimore, 1837.

Mackie, John Milton. *From Cape Cod to Dixie and the Tropics*. New York, 1864.

Macleod, William. *Harper's New York and Erie Rail-Road Guide Book*. New York, 1852. Several eds.

Marcy, Randolph B. *The Prairie Traveller: A Handbook for Overland Expeditions*. New York, 1859.

Marvin, Henry. *A Complete History of Lake George: Embracing a Great Variety of Information . . . with an especial reference to meet the wants of the Traveling Community. . . .* New York, 1853.

Marx, Leo. *The Machine in the Garden.* New York, 1964.

McConnel, J. L. *Western Characters, or, Types of Border Life in the Western States.* 1853.

McDermott, John Francis, ed. *Research Opportunities in American Cultural History.* Lexington, Ky., 1961. This contains an excellent chapter on travel literature by Thomas D. Clark.

Mather, Cotton. *Magnalia Christi Americana.* 1702.

Mellen, Grenville. *A Book of the United States.* Hartford, 1842.

Melville, Herman. *The Confidence-Man.* 1857.
———. *Redburn.* 1849.
———. *Moby Dick.* 1851.

Midgley, R. L. *Sights in Boston and Suburbs.* Boston, 1856.

Milburn, William Henry. *The Rifle, Axe, and Saddle-Bags, and other lectures.* New York, 1857.

Mitchell, Samuel Augustus. *Illinois in 1837.* Philadelphia, 1837.

Moore, Arthur K. *The Frontier Mind.* New York, 1963.

Morrison, Thomas. *The Traveller's Companion.* Philadelphia, [1830].

Nason, Daniel. *A Journal of a Tour from Boston to Savannah, Thence to Havana . . . Thence to New Orleans and Several Western Cities. . . .* Cambridge, Mass., 1849.

Nelsons' [sic] *Illustrated Guide to the Hudson.* New York, 1860.

Nevins, Allan, ed. *American Social History as Recorded by British Travellers.* New York, 1923.

Nichols, Thomas Law. *Forty Years of American Life 1821–61.* New York, 1937. First published 1864.

[Nicklin, Philip H.] *A Pleasant Peregrination through the Prettiest Parts of Pennsylvania.* Philadelphia, 1836.

Nye, Russell B. *The Unembarrassed Muse: The Popular Arts in America.* New York, 1970.

————. *Notes on a Rationale for Popular Culture.* Popular Culture Association, 1971.

Oakes, William. *Oakes' White Mountain Scenery.* 1848.

Olmsted, Frederick Law. *A Journey in the Seaboard Slave States.* New York, 1856.

Orr, J. W. *Pictorial Guide to the Falls of Niagara: A Manual for Visitors.* Buffalo, 1842.

Parker, Henry. *Stranger's Guide Book to Mount Auburn Cemetery.* Boston, 1849.

Parker, Nathan Howe. *Iowa as It Is in 1856.* Chicago, 1856.
————. *Iowa as It Is in 1857.* Chicago, 1857.

Parker, Samuel. *Journal of an Exploring Tour beyond the Rocky Mountains.* 1838.

Parkman, Francis. *The Oregon Trail.* New York, 1950. New American Library ed. First published 1849.

Parsons, Horatio. *Book of Niagara Falls.* Buffalo, 1836. Several eds.

Pattie, James O. *The Personal Narrative.* Philadelphia, 1962. Unabridged 1831 ed.

[Paulding, James K.] *The New Mirror for Travellers, and Guide to the Springs.* New York, 1828.

Paulding, James K. *Letters from the South.* 2 vols. New York, 1835.

Pearce, Roy Harvey. *The Savages of America.* Baltimore, 1953.

Peck, John Mason. *A New Guide for Emigrants.* Boston, 1836.

Pecks' [sic] *Tourist's Companion to Niagara Falls, Sarasota Springs, the Lakes, Canada, etc.* Buffalo, 1845.

Phelps' Hundred Cities and Large Towns of America. New York, 1853.

Philadelphia as It Is, in 1852. Philadelphia, 1852.

The Picturesque Pocket Companion and Visitor's Guide through Mount Auburn. Boston, 1839.

Plumbe, John, Jr. *Sketches of Iowa and Wisconsin.* 1948. Rpt. of 1839 ed. Despite title, covers Iowa only.

Redpath, James, and Richard J. Hinton. *Handbook to Kansas Territory and the Rocky Mountains Gold Region, etc.* New York, 1859.

Revere, Joseph. *A Tour of Duty in California.* New York, 1849.

Richards, T[homas] Addison. *American Scenery, Illustrated.* New York, 1854.

————. *Appleton's Illustrated Hand-Book of American Travel: Southern and Western States and the Territories.* New York, 1857.

————. *Appleton's Companion Hand-Book of Travel.* New York, 1860.

Rourke, Constance. *American Humor.* New York, 1931.

Royall, Anne. *Mrs. Royall's Pennsylvania, or, Travels Continued in the United States.* Washington, D.C., 1829.

[————.] *Sketches of History, Life, and Manners in the United States.* New Haven, 1826.

Rusk, Ralph L. *The Literature of the Middle Western Frontier.* 2 vols. New York, 1925.

Sanford, Charles L. *The Quest for Paradise.* Urbana, Illinois, 1961.

Sanford, Charles L., ed. *The Quest for America 1810–1824.* New York, 1964.

Santayana, George. *Character and Opinion in the United States.* New York, 1934.

Schoolcraft, Henry Rowe. *Narrative of an Expedition through the Upper Mississippi . . .* 1834.

Sears, Robert. *A Pictorial Description of the United States.* New York, 1860.

Seltzer, L. E., ed. *Columbia Lippincott Gazetteer of the World.* New York, 1852.

Sewall, R. K. *Sketches of St. Augustine.* New York, 1848.

Seymour, E. S. *Sketches of Minnesota, the New England of the West.* New York, 1850.

Sherman, John. *Trenton Falls, Picturesque and Descriptive.* Ed. Nathaniel Parker Willis. New York, 1851. Willis inserted his own descriptions of Trenton Falls in this book, but Sherman's 1827 essay was primarily used in my analysis.

Shepard, Paul. *Man in the Landscape.* New York, 1967.

Shillaber, B[enjamin] P[enhallow]. *Life and Saynigs of Mrs. Partington. . . .* New York, 1854.

Shortfield, Luke. *The Western Merchant: . . . Hints for those who Design Emigrating to the West. Deduced from Actual Experience*. Philadelphia, 1849.

Simms, William Gilmore. "Summer Travel in the South," *Southern Quarterly Review*, 18, n.s. 2 (September 1850): 26–27.

Simpson, Henry J. *The Emigrant's Guide to the Gold Mines*. New York, 1848.

Smith, Henry Nash. *Virgin Land*. New York, 1950.

Smith, John Calvin. *Western Tourist and Emigrant's Guide*. New York, 1846.

————. *The Illustrated Hand-Book: A New Guide for Travellers through the United States*. New York, 1846.

Smith, Preserved. *Origins of Modern Culture*. New York, 1934. Rpt. 1962.

Smith, R. A. *Smith's Illustrated Guide to and through Laurel Hill Cemetery*. 1852.

Spaulding, John H. *Historical Relics of the White Mountains. Also, A Concise White Mountain Guide. . . .* Boston, 1855.

Springer, John S. *Forest Life and Forest Trees*. New York, 1851. Thoreau referred to this book in *The Maine Woods* (1864).

Steele, Elisa R. *A Summer Journey in the West*. New York, 1841.

Steele, John. *The Traveler's Companion through the Interior*. Galena, Ill., 1854.

Steele, Oliver G. *Steele's Western Guide Book and Emigrant's Directory*. Buffalo, 1835.

Stiff, Col. Edward. *The Texas Emigrant*. Cincinnati, 1840.

The Stranger's Guide to Baltimore. . . . By a Baltimorean. Baltimore, 1852.

Strickland, W. P. *The Pioneers of the West, or, Life in the Woods*. New York, 1856.

Our Summer Retreats. New York, 1858.

Taft, Kendall B., ed. *Minor Knickerbocker*. New York, 1947.

Tanner, Henry S. *View of the Valley of the Mississippi*. Philadelphia, 1834.

————. *The American Traveller*. Philadelphia, 1834.

————. *The American Traveller,* Philadelphia, 1839.

Taylor, Bayard. *Eldorado, or, Adventures in the Path of Empire.* New York, 1868. First published 1850.

————. *At Home and Abroad: A Sketch-Book of Life, Scenery, and Men.* New York, 1860.

Taylor, William. *California Life Illustrated.* New York, 1860.

Taylor, William R. *Cavalier and Yankee.* New York, 1963.

Thomas, G. F., ed. *Appleton's Railway and Steam Navigation Guide . . . A Commercial Register.* New York, [1850].

[Thompson, William T.] *Major Jones's Sketches of Travel.* 1848.

Thoreau, Henry David. *A Week on the Concord and Merrimack Rivers.* 1849.

————. *Walden.* 1854.

Thwaites, Reuben G., ed. *Early Western Travels 1748–1846. . . .* 32 vols. Cleveland, 1904–07. Includes foreign as well as American travels.

Tocqueville, Alexis de. *Democracy in America.* Ed. Phillips Bradley, 2 vols. New York, 1954. First American ed. 1838.

The Tourist, or, Pocket Manual for Travellers on the Hudson River. . . . New York, 1841.

Tower, F. B. *Illustrations of the Croton Aqueduct.* New York, 1843.

The Traveller's Directory and Emigrant's Guide. Buffalo, 1832.

Traveller's Guide and Emigrant's Directory through the States of Ohio, Illinois, Indiana, and Michigan. New York, 1836.

Trollope, Frances. *Domestic Manners of the Americans.* Ed. Donald Smalley. New York, 1960. First published 1832.

Tryon, Warren S., ed. *A Mirror for Americans: Life and Manners in the United States 1790–1870 as Recorded by American Travelers.* 3 vols. Chicago, 1952. This anthology contains a very good introduction to and bibliography of travel books.

Tuckerman, Henry T. *America and Her Commentators, with a Critical Sketch of Travel in the United States.* New York, 1961. First published 1864, but publication was planned as early as February, 1862 under the title *Travels and Travellers in America.*

[Vandewater, R. J.] *The Tourist, or, Pocket Manual for Travellers on the Hudson River, the Western Canal, and State Road, etc.* New York, 1830.

Walter, Cornelia. *Mount Auburn Illustrated.* New York, [1848].

Ware, Joseph. *The Emigrants' Guide to California.* 1849. Rpt. 1932.

Warner, I. W. *The Immigrant's Guide and Citizen's Manual: A Work for Immigrants of all Classes . . . with Directions and Valuable Information for Travellers.* New York, 1848.

The Western Traveler's Pocket Directory and Stranger's Guide. Schenectady, 1836.

Wetmore, Alphonso. *Gazetteers of the State of Missouri.* St. Louis, 1837.

Whipple, Edwin P. *Character and Characteristic Men.* Boston, 1866. This book includes a study of the national character written and published in the antebellum period.

Whitman, Walt. *Leaves of Grass.* 1855.

Willey, Benjamin G. *Incidents in White Mountain History . . . to which is added an Accurate Guide from New York and Boston to the White Mountains.* Boston, 1856.

Williams, John Lee. *The Territory of Florida.* New York, 1837. Facsimile rpt., introduction by Herbert J. Doherty, Jr., 1962.

Williams, Wellington. *Appleton's Northern and Eastern Traveller's Guide.* New York, 1852.

———. *Appleton's Southern and Western Traveller's Guide.* New York, 1854.

———. *Appleton's New and Complete United States Guide Book for Travellers.* New York, 1854.

———. *Appleton's Railroad and Steamboat Companion.* New York, 1847.

Willis, Nathaniel Parker. *Health Trip to the Tropics.* New York, 1853.

———. *Hurry-Graphs, or, Sketches of Scenery, Celebrities,*

and Society, Taken from Life, Auburn and Rochester, N.Y., 1856. First published 1851.

Wilson, Edmund, ed. *The Shock of Recognition.* New York, 1943. Rpt. 1955.

[Wilson, Henry.] *Wilson's Illustrated Guide to the Hudson River.* New York, 1851. Several eds.

[Wines, Enoch C.] *A Trip to Boston. . . .* Boston, 1838.

Winthrop, Theodore. *Life in the Open Air.* Boston, 1863. An account of antebellum travel published posthumously.

Wise, Henry A. *Los Gringas, or, an Inside View of Mexico and California. . . .* 1849.

Wright, Louis B. *Culture on the Moving Frontier.* New York, 1961.

INDEX